Exploring Consumer Traits Online Market

James M. Allen

Abstract

Emerging technology and online environments have contributed to significant growth in the online knowledge market and entrepreneurs have begun to build businesses in the digital arena selling knowledge as a product. This study addressed the question of how personality traits impact the consumer's perceived value of online paid knowledge (OPK) products. The purpose of this qualitative analysis was to address how personality traits impact consumers' perceptions of value with online paid knowledge (OPK) products. Further, exploration of how these constructs form patterns that explain the perceived usefulness and perceived ease of use of OPK products, specifically online courses, of consumers in the U.S. from 2018–2021. Using a case study design, the conceptual framework for the study included the technology acceptance model (TAM) and the five-factor model (FFM) of personality traits. The researcher analyzed responses from 22 semi-structured interviews through an inductive thematic analysis approach. The following four themes emerged from the research questions: *personality factors via OPK characteristics, perceived ease of use via platform characteristics, perceived usefulness by a value of OPK, and use of OPK via challenges of OPK.* Findings showed agreeableness as the dominant personality trait for three of the themes and conscientiousness for one of the four themes. The findings expanded previous literature by providing a better understanding of how consumer personality traits affected the perceived value of online paid knowledge products within the context of perceived usefulness and perceived ease of use among consumers in the United States. Recommendations for future research include the impact of consumer use when observed using a framework(s) other than TAM or FFM; assessing the role of accountability and

i

credibility of the course or instructor, as well as researching the study with a quantitative methodology. The potential implications of the results in practice for digital entrepreneurs may become significant aspects influencing the marketing strategies in the OPK market based on personality traits. Additionally, market research of consumers' personality traits aids in predictive capabilities of perceived usefulness and perceived ease of use.

Table of Contents

Chapter 1: Introduction 1

    Statement of the Problem 4
    Purpose of the Study 5
    Introduction to Theoretical Framework 6
    Introduction to Research Methodology and Design 9
    Research Questions 11
    Significance of the Study 12
    Definitions of Key Terms 13
    Summary 15

Chapter 2: Literature Review 16

    Theoretical Framework Overview 17
    Summary of Seminal Research 18
    The Technology Acceptance Model (TAM) 20
    Foundational Theories and Evolution of TAM 24
    Additional Theories Related to Behavior and Technology 25
    Criticism of TAM 28
    TAM Studied in Various Settings 28
    TAM and Online Shopping 30
    TAM Researched in Knowledge Sharing 31
    TAM in Online Learning 32
    Five-Factor Model (FFM) of Personality 33
    FFM Used in Consumer Behavior Research 36
    FFM Research in Online Shopping 38
    FFM Research in Online Learning 39
    FFM Research in Usability 40
    Critiques of the FFM 41
    Five-Factor Model (FFM) of Personality Traits in this study 42
    TAM Studied With FFM 42
    Development of Online Learning Relevant to Current Study 47
    Massive Open Online Courses (MOOCs) Studied With TAM: A Predecessor to OPK 48
    From Free to Paid 54
    Online Paid Knowledge (OPK) Market 64
    Application of TAM and FFM to Current Study 69
    Summary 71

Chapter 3: Research Method 75

    Research Methodology and Design 76
    Qualitative Method For this Study 81
    Boundaries of Case Study 84
    Population and Sample 84

Materials 86

Study Procedures 89

Data Collection and Analysis.. 91

Assumptions... 93

Limitations 94

Delimitations.. 95

Ethical Assurances 95

Summary 97

Chapter 4: Findings... 99

Trustworthiness of the Data 100

Results... 102

Steps Taken to Analyze the Data 105

Resultant Themes from the Analysis 115

Evaluation of Findings... 133

Research Question 1 and Research Question 2 Aligned by Theme................... 134

Summary 139

Chapter 5: Implications, Recommendations, and Conclusions 141

Implications of Themes by Research Questions.. 142

Recommendations for Future Research and Practice 151

Limitations and Recommendations for Research and Practice............................ 157

Conclusions... 157

List of Tables

Table 1 *Study Participants by Gender Identity, Personality* 102

Table 2 *Codes, Examples, Direct Quotations, and Counts* 107

Table 3 *From Codes to Categories* 110

Table 4 *From Categories to Themes* 114

Table 5 *Research Questions by Theme* 134

Table 6 *Shared Concepts: Research Question 1 and Theme 1* 135

Table 7 *Shared Concepts: Research Question 1 and Theme 4* 136

Table 8 *Shared Concepts: Research Question 2 and Theme 2* 138

Table 9 *Shared Concepts: Research Question 2 and Theme 3* 138

List of Figures

Figure 1 *Theme One: Personality Factors via OPK Characteristics* 117
Figure 2 *Theme One by Personality Type, Participant Count* 119
Figure 3 *Theme Two: Perceived Ease of Use (PEOU) via Platform Characteristics* 121
Figure 4 *Theme Two by Personality Type, Participant Count* 124
Figure 5 *Theme Three: Perceived Usefulness (PU) via Value of OPK* 125
Figure 6 *Theme Three by Personality Type, Participant Count* 128
Figure 7 *Theme Four: Use of OPK via Challenges of OPK* 129
Figure 8 *Theme Four by Personality Type, Participant Count* 133

Chapter 1: Introduction

Online knowledge platforms, such as webinars, have become a key source of marketing, product promotion, teleconferencing meetings, and training programs (Herrhausen et al., 2020; Hsiao, 2020). Webinars are among the top five marketing tools, and 46% of United States companies use webinars (Kannan & Li, 2017). Companies that use webinars in the United States as marketing tools include Amazon, Adobe, and Goldman Sachs. Previous research has focused on the use of knowledge content in webinars by digital entrepreneurs in the context of marketing tools and brand development to increase brand awareness, create more leads, and increase loyalty among customers (Alford et al., 2015; Gebauer et al., 2020; Gregori, 2020; Kannan & Li, 2017; Said et al., 2020).

Online knowledge platforms are also used as a learning facilitator for digital content. (Cai et al., 2020). With technological advances and the demand for knowledge, the knowledge industry has become complex in the digital world (Cai et al., 2020). The digital knowledge content industry began around 2001 with OpenCourseWare publishing courses on the Internet. Several iterations later, massive open online courses (MOOC) were developed in 2008 and used by traditional institutions to offer free courses through an online learning platform (Liyanagunawardena et al., 2013). Online courses are experiencing a transformation from free knowledge to online paid knowledge (OPK) (Reyna, 2020; Su et al., 2019; Zhang et al., 2019). Cai et al. (2020) indicated a high demand for knowledge today, and online courses are a way of self-education and range from specific topics like technology skills to broader topics, such as self-improvement and travel (Zhang et al., 2019). The digital content industry has seen exponential growth since 2015, with growth rates ranging between 24%–40% (Aswani et al., 2018; Lim et al., 2016; Zhang et al., 2019; Zhang et al., 2020). In 2020, the size and scope of the information economy, including segments such as music, videos, news, and books, was estimated to be $14.5 billion in the United States (Hofacker et al., 2020).

The paid knowledge content market has begun to represent a significant category in this industry (Dou et al., 2013; Zhang et al., 2019). For example, Coursera, a well-known course provider in the United States, boasted a 444% increase in course sales in 2019, with Forbes valuing them at $7 billion (Coursera, 2020; Zhang et al., 2020). In countries such as China, the volume of consumers willing to pay for online knowledge products exceeded $3.46 billion in 2020 (Fang et al., 2021; Su et al., 2019). Because the industry is new and fast developing, there is an inconsistency in terms used to describe and define the market.

There have been attempts to create a framework to classify digital products by categories and characteristics (Hui, 2002; Ivanisin, 2012). However, there are inconsistencies with terms used for online knowledge products in research. Jing (2020) stated that the online knowledge product and knowledge content industry are challenging to define. Clarifying the terms used in this market aids in understanding the framework for this study. Appendix A contains a non-exhaustive list of terms used in research sources to describe this market. The size and scope of the information economy are vast, and Hofacker et al. (2020) attempted to identify the variety of products in this industry by separating them into categories of goods and services. Hofacker et al. (2020) attempted to define the term "information products" in literature, stating, "Our definition closely matches Meyer and Zack (1996) and Tiwana and Ramesh (2001), who define information products as interdependent and intangible packages of information capable of distribution in digital form."

Due to the complexity of technology and the speed of advancement, the OPK industry has received limited research in businesses, including strategies to promote knowledge as a product (Ivanova, 2018; Kannan & Li, 2017; Kimura, 2018). While the statistics above suggest the OPK market usage continues to increase, there is limited information about strategies marketers use to design and promote online knowledge products, such as paid courses and information products, and not as an advert for a company or an individual (Agarwal, 2015; Zhang et al., 2019; Zhang et al., 2020).

Literature regarding knowledge products has primarily focused on free online knowledge sharing (Altalhi, 2021; Fu et al., 2020; Littenberg-Tobias et al., 2020; Su et al., 2018; Zhang et al., 2019), as well as the diffusion of innovations in technology and digital transformation of products from online stores (Berman, 2012; Bucko et al., 2018; Hofacker et al., 2020). Personality traits in the context of consumer behavior have been widely studied (Bosnjak et al., 2007; Chen, 2011; Du et al., 2021; McElroy et al., 2007; Pflugner et al., 2020), as well as the relationship between personality traits and online shopping (Aldousari et al., 2016; Bawack et al., 2021; Bosnjak et al., 2007; Huang et al., 2010; Usakli, 2019; Watjatrakul 2020). More specifically, there have been multiple studies relating the five-factor model (FFM) of personality traits to technology models, such as the unified theory of acceptance and use of technology (UTAUT; Lakhal et al., 2017; Svendsen et al., 2013), the 3M motivational model (Bahl et al., 2019; Bento et al., 2019) and technology acceptance model (TAM) (Barnett et al., 2015; Devaraj et al., 2008; Harb et al., 2019).

Entrepreneurs have taken advantage of the opportunities in emerging technology and online environments and have begun to build businesses in the digital arena (Fang et al., 2021; Kraus et al., 2018; Scott et al., 2019). An increasing number of digital entrepreneurs use online platforms to produce and sell their knowledge and content as an end product (Cai et al., 2020; Su et al., 2019). Su et al. (2019) underscored that presenting OPK platforms as products and not services to customers is an important way to increase revenue for the merchants participating in the OPK market. However, consumers' attitudes and intentions to purchase digital knowledge products are unclear, and there is a lack of knowledge regarding the determinates of sales in the OPK market (Fu et al., 2020; Zhang et al., 2020; Zhang et al., 2020). Personality traits and OPK characteristics have significantly influenced consumers' perceived value (Watjatrakul, 2020). Investigating how different personality traits respond to OPK product characteristics (system quality, information quality, service quality) may impact digital entrepreneurs' marketing strategies and design. The evidence reviewed above suggests that the OPK market plays a crucial role for digital entrepreneurs (Jin, 2020; Watjatrakul, 2020).

Statement of the Problem

The problem in this study addressed the question of how personality traits of consumers perceive value of OPK products using perceived usefulness (PU) and perceived ease of use (PEOU) as constructs among consumers in the United States (Bahl et al., 2019; Fu et al., 2020; Jin et al., 2020; Jing et al., 2020; Seibert et al., 2021; Su et al., 2019). Su et al. (2019) cited the need for further inquiry to understand how perceived value in the OPK market is affected by personality traits. Similarly, Bahl et al. (2019) and Seibert et al. (2021) expressed a need for further research on more specific technologies related to personality traits rather than technology in general. Several studies have called for further research on the TAM model, including investigating user perspectives in e-learning (Mohammadi, 2015) and further exploration of product characteristics: service quality, information quality, and system quality (Jin, 2020). In a study on knowledge products in China, Fu et al. (2020) suggested future research on knowledge products and consumer satisfaction from other countries. Failure to understand personality traits within the constructs of OPK characteristics as well as their perception of value could result in failed marketing strategies among digital entrepreneurs as competition in the OPK market

continues to grow (Beig et al., 2019; Fu et al., 2020; Kraus, 2018; Marbach et al., 2016;

Matarazzo, 2021; Su et al., 2019).

Many studies have focused on online shopping behavior, including willingness to

purchase (Berger et al., 2015; Bucko et al., 2018; Li et al., 2017; Rajani, 2019). Purchase

intention factors, such as perceived risk (Biucky et al., 2017), perceived value (Gvili et al.,

2020), and perceived use (Ha et al., 2019), are a few topics researched in the online market.

Agarwal (2015) and Huang (2016) researched e-commerce within the technology adoption

framework. Watjatakul (2020) determined that different personality traits affect the perceived

value and intention to adopt online courses. However, there is limited research in the literature

exploring personality traits and technology interaction with digital learning products sold by for-

profit businesses (Bento et al., 2019; Bruso et al., 2020; Regele, 2020; Zhou, 2022). This study

sought to address this problem by discussing how personality factors (agreeableness, openness,

conscientiousness, neuroticism and extroversion) impact consumer's perceived value, PU, and

PEOU within the contextual antecedents of OPK product characteristics (Goldberg, 1990; Jin,

2020; Watjatrakul, 2020).

Purpose of the Study

The purpose of this qualitative case study was to address how different personality traits

describe value within the constructs of PU and PEOU of online courses in the OPK market using

the contextual antecedents of OPK characteristics of consumers in the United States from 2018–

2021. Usakli (2019) called for further research on personality traits in online shopping using a

qualitative method. They further suggested that studies should be expanded beyond higher

education and use participants other than predominantly students in research. Zhou et al. (2022)

suggested that future studies focus on consumer characteristics in electronic commerce. Understanding a consumer's personality traits within the OPK market constructs of OPK product characteristics helps identify consumer preferences and their PU and PEOU (Barnett, 2015).

A qualitative methodology provided a more in-depth perception of consumers' attitudes toward online courses and their characteristics. The individual experiences and perceptions captured in the case study design provided insights into their PU and PEOU. Firms that can create value propositions with the characteristics of their OPK products and customize their promotion to fit the personality traits of their preferred customer will have a competitive advantage in the marketplace (Jin et al., 2020; Marbach et al., 2016; Najafabadi et al., 2020; Watjatrakul, 2020).

Semi-structured interviews collected the required data from 22 participants. The interviews consisted of open-ended questions to elicit data relevant to addressing the study problem. Videoconference interviews (such as Zoom) ensured the safety of the researcher and participants while social-distancing guidelines related to the Covid-19 pandemic were in place (Gray et al., 2020). This explorative study adds to the body of research by extending the previous research of the FFM and the TAM model to include OPK product characteristics of the digital content industry. Additionally, providing a qualitative analysis allowed for additional insights that a quantitative study would normally not capture due to the nature of the analysis (Braun & Clark, 2006; Galletta, 2013; Merriam et al., 2016, Usakli, 2019).

Introduction to Theoretical Framework

This study used the technology acceptance model (TAM) as a guiding framework and the five-factor model (FFM) of personality traits as constructs (Davis, 1989; Costa et al., 1987; Svendsen et al., 2013; Usakli, 2019). The guiding framework used a thematic analysis approach.

It consisted of consumer personality factors and OPK product antecedents that were examined to understand the impact on PU and PEOU and the consumer's perception of value. Perceived value motivates us and has shown that it influences behavioral intention (Braun & Clarke, 2006; Belotto, 2018; Chen et al., 2008; Gao, 2021; Gronroos, 2013). Therefore, thematic analysis is an excellent way to discover how different personality traits perceive value within the TAM model (Braun & Clark, 2006; Strifler et al., 2020).

TAM, established in 1989, is a well-established theory when studying technology and online behavioral intention and has been chosen because of the two main components (PU and PEOU). Therefore, this serves as a valuable framework for understanding the impact of personality trait factors and the characteristics of OPK products (Barnett, 2015; Davis, 1989; Devaraj, 2008; Harb, 2019; Su et al., 2019; Wu, 2015). Furthermore, as perceived value influences behavioral intention, TAM is a reliable model for the current study (Gao, 2021).

As an extension of the theory of reasoned action (TRA) designed by Ajzen (1991), TAM explains behavioral intention within the context of PU, PEOU and attitude towards its use. Perceived value as an attitude is a significant factor in purchase behavior and was analyzed in the model (Aldousari et al., 2016; Chen et al., 2008; Chen et al., 2019; Davis, 1989; Gao, 2021; Gvili et al., 2019; Li et al., 2017; Su et al., 2019; Watjatrakul, 2018; Zhu, 2019). PU describes how the technology product will help the consumer. Finally, PEOU defines how much effort is required on the part of the consumer. (Aldousari et al., 2016; Altalhi, 2021; Bucko et al., 2018; Davis, 1989).

Previous research has used personality traits as moderators and predictors of TAM (Barnett, 2015; Costa et al., 1987; Harb, 2019; Lakhal, 2017; Su, 2019; Svendsen et al., 2013; Usakli, 2019; Watjatrakul, 2020; Wu, 2015). Personality traits reflect the nature of a person and typically what they value in terms of PU and PEOU. The research demonstrates the use of TAM and served as a frame of reference in developing the research questions (Devaraj et al., 2008; Gvili et al., 2019; Marbach et al., 2016). The FFM has been used to predict consumer behavior and includes these factors: extraversion, neuroticism, agreeableness, conscientiousness, and openness to experience (Chen et al., 2008; Goldberg, 1990; Watjatrakul, B., 2020). The FFM test, also known as the "big five," is an ideal concept for this study as it provides a reliable, succinct evaluation of the personality traits of the participant (Boyle, 2008; Caprara, 1993; Costa et al., 1987; Goldberg, 1990; PsychTests AIM, I., 2011,Usakli, 2019).

OPK characteristics are described in different ways according to the researcher's objective. One method is descriptors, such as functional, emotional, and social value (Burucuoglu et al., 2016; Su et al., 2019). However, this study used antecedents of system quality, information quality, and service quality (Altalhi, 2021; Jin, 2020; Jing, 2020). These antecedents contribute to technology adoption and consumer perceived value (Panigrahi et al., 2018).

Research involving FFM and TAM is not a new concept (Harb et al., 2019; Svendsen et al., 2013). However, there is a gap in the literature regarding the impact of personality traits in the OPK sector of the digital content industry (Su et al., 2019; Usakli, 2019). As personality traits are what we do, value is what motivates the consumer. Value is not created by the provider but by the relationship between the provider and the consumer. It is not defined by the product's price but rather by what is received (Gronroos, 2013). The framework addressed personality factors while describing the personal experience and perception of the value of PU and PEOU of online courses.

Introduction to Research Methodology and Design

A qualitative methodology guided this research. A qualitative descriptive construct is a functional methodological design that researchers can use to describe realities about a given phenomenon described by the selected participants (Yin, 2015). Qualitative research methodologies are effective when researchers intend to collect information through case studies using semi-structured interviews and surveys to address the "how," "what," and "when" questions that provide a deeper understanding of the problem (Huyler et al., 2019; Yin, 2015).

Researchers can provide precise descriptions through qualitative analysis that may help attach meaning to the research and give a deeper understanding of the phenomenon other than understanding quantitative data (Koh et al., 2000; Merriam, 2016). According to Dulock (1993), a case study design allows investigators to explore human experience complexities while allowing for common realities. Therefore, using a qualitative case study design was appropriate for the current study because it aimed to capture the experience of consumers and address how different personality traits may impact consumer's PU and PEOU within the contextual antecedents of OPK characteristics (Goldberg, 1990; Jin, 2020; Watjatrakul, 2020). In addition, this approach allowed for thematic analysis and helped make connections between factors and antecedents, particularly in reference to the perceived value within non-academic settings (Braun & Clark., 2006; Bruso et al., 2020; Castleberry and Nolen, 2018; Lambert et al., 2012; Thomas, 2018).

To better understand the contextual information on the personality traits and characteristics of OPK products, the researcher used a case study research design that integrated interviews and surveys as a method to understand and describe the personality traits of OPK consumers and the antecedents of OPK course characteristics. By describing this phenomenon in its natural setting, using inductive thematic analysis, a deeper understanding of personality traits and characteristics of OPK courses surfaced in the data (Braun, 2021; Spiers et al., 2019). The study included triangulation using literature analysis, semi-structured interviews, and data collection of consumers who have purchased online knowledge products from 2018–2021. The semi-structured interviews captured additional dimensions of the consumer's perception of OPK characteristics and survey personality traits. The sample size totaled 22 participants and was sufficient to reach data saturation (Hennink & Kaiser, 2022; Stake, 2010). A purposeful sampling technique ensured that the exploration provided an understanding of course interactions from each of the "big five" personality traits (Kalu, 2019). Additionally, it allowed for ease of replication of the study by providing an unbiased sampling.

The interviews were audio-recorded using the videoconference application's audio-recording feature to ensure accurate data reporting (Gray et al., 2020). Data was validated through member checking of transcripts. The recordings of the interviews were transcribed verbatim, and the transcripts were imported into computer-assisted qualitative data analysis software (e.g., NiVivo 12) for thematic analysis to identify overarching themes in participants' descriptions. Additional data was collected by a questionnaire completed before the interview as a pre-study approach to obtain demographic information and knowledge regarding participants' personality traits via close-ended demographic questions and a personality assessment questionnaire, such as the FFM of personality scale. The five-factor personality assessment has been shown to achieve a more accurate response from participants than live questions, as people are more likely, to be honest in their self-evaluation in this format (Bahcekapili, 2020; Costa et al., 1987; Harb, 2019).

The data collection procedure began with the researcher seeking approval from Northcentral's University Institutional Review Board. After approval, the researcher sought consumers in the OPK market. Next, participants were invited to the study through flyers, email, social messaging, and word of mouth. Eligible participants signed an informed consent form before participating in the study. Next, participants participated in a survey/questionnaire before the interview to collect demographic information and complete a personality assessment. They participated in 45–60 minutes of a recorded interview via Zoom. Data analysis was the next step after the researcher had transcribed all interviews. The analysis used an inductive thematic analysis process (Braun & Clark, 2006).

Research Questions

The findings of this qualitative inquiry aimed to address personality factors (agreeableness, openness, conscientiousness, neuroticism and extroversion) and contextual antecedents of OPK characteristics (system quality, information quality and service quality) and how these constructs form patterns that explain PU and PEOU of OPK products, specifically online courses (Goldberg, 1990; Jin, 2020; Watjatrakul, 2020). The objective of the research questions was to analyze different personality traits and OPK characteristics and how they lead to perceived value using the constructs of PU and PEOU ease of use of OPK products.

RQ1

How do the five personality trait factors (agreeableness, openness, neuroticism, conscientiousness, extroversion) impact consumer perception of online course characteristics (system quality, information quality, service quality)?

RQ2

How do the five personality trait factors (agreeableness, openness, neuroticism, conscientiousness, extroversion) and the online course characteristics (system quality, information quality, service quality) affect consumer perceived value using the constructs of perceived usefulness (PU) and perceived ease of use (PEOU)?

Significance of the Study

The study aimed to extend the body of literature by addressing gaps in consumer behavior in the online shopping industry within the construct of online courses in the digital content industry. Studies of online shopping include pricing strategies for online knowledge products as well as technology adoption (Balasubramanian et al., 2015; Cai et al., 2020; Dou, 2020; Greenstein et al., 2012; Li et al., 2019; Lin et al., 2020; RuBell et al., 2020; Zhang et al., 2008). Previous research includes the general topic of personality traits and technology adoption (Barnett et al., 2015; Svendsen et al., 2013). This study extended the literature on the TAM model and served as a background for the theoretical framework through an inductive thematic analysis of the research questions (Aldousari, 2016; Davis, 1989). TRA and TAM propose that external factors, such as personal characteristics, affect behavioral intention by impacting attitude. This study discussed the relevance of the literature regarding these two factors in the OPK industry (Aldousari et al., 2016; Venkatesh, 2002).

The practical implications of this study for business practice included the insight to address the practice of designing, marketing, and product promotion issues targeting specific consumers' personality traits in OPK courses. The exploration could increase sales and facilitate webinars' suitability and online courses over rival products (Gregori et al., 2020; Herrhausen et al., 2020; Hofacker et al., 2020). Study findings may be valuable to digital entrepreneurs concerned with marketing webinars and online courses by understanding different personality factors and their impact on perceived value and forming the best strategies that appeal to consumers in various markets and business needs. With the proper positioning of the online course in the OPK market, a small business will likely use its platform to reach new markets that would directly increase the market base, sales, and profitability. Such information can help understand the key factors influencing the purchase of webinars and online courses. The information could also help digital entrepreneurs develop online courses differently based on consumer personality traits and demographics and create a positioning strategy in the market (Amakiri, 2019; Antonopoulou, 2020; Hsieh et al., 2019; Kraus, 2018; Ludeke-Freund, 2020, Park et al., 2020).

Definitions of Key Terms

Key terms are listed here. As there is a lack of consistency with terms in this industry, Appendix A contains a more detailed list of terms for the knowledge market, along with references where terms have been used in prior research.

Digital Content

Digital Content is described as various types of material utilizing digital technology distributed through various platforms (Yeh, 2017).

Digital Entrepreneurship

Digital Entrepreneurship is a subcategory of entrepreneurship describing business in the digital era specifically operated on the Internet (Kraus et al., 2018).

Digital Marketing

Digital Marketing is a subcategory of marketing describing the marketing of products using a digital channel (Kannan & Li, 2017).

Marketing

Marketing refers to a company promoting the buying or selling of a product or service (Gegenfurtner et al., 2020).

Massive Open Online Courses (MOOC)

Massive open online courses are free and open use of knowledge in the form of digital content, often funded through supportive online systems such as educational systems (Vorbach, 2019).

Online Paid Knowledge (OPK)

Online paid knowledge refers to transactions occurring on online platforms. These may include communities where buyers and sellers share, seek, and buy knowledge through Q&A sites and course platforms (Su et al., 2019).

Perceived Usefulness (PU)

One of the two primary constructs in the technology acceptance model (TAM), perceived usefulness is defined as, "the degree to which a person believes that using a particular system would enhance his or her job performance" (Abdullah, F. et al., 2016; Davis, 1989).

Perceived Usefulness (PU)

The second construct in the technology acceptance model, perceived ease of use (PEOU) is defined as, "the degree to which a person believes that using a particular system would be free of effort" (Abdullah, F. et al., 2016; Davis, 1989).

Webinars

Webinars are a form of conferencing that entails a seminar offered over the Internet (Gegenfurtner et al., 2019; Reissis et al., 2020).

Summary

Personality traits and technology adoption coupled with OPK characteristics, such as system quality, information quality, and service quality, have become significant aspects influencing the marketing strategies digital entrepreneurs use by focusing on the design and marketing of such platforms, including webinars (Reyna et al., 2020; Su et al., 2019, Usakli, 2019). This study aimed to address the lack of understanding of personality traits and OPK characteristics in the OPK market among consumers in the United States (Bahl et al., 2019, Bento et al., 2019, Fu et al., 2020; Jing et al., 2020; Su et al., 2019; Su et al., 2018; Yildiz et al., 2020). Firms that can create value propositions with the characteristics of their OPK product and customize their promotion to fit the personality traits of their preferred customer will have a competitive advantage in the marketplace (Jin et al., 2020; Gronroos, 2013; Najafabadi et al., 2020; Watjatrakul, 2020). This case study addressed how personality traits and OPK characteristics impact perceived value and used a qualitative case study analysis to understand the consumer's PU and PEOU of online courses in the OPK industry (Zhang et al., 2020). Chapter 2 provides an overview of the theoretical framework and literature that supports this study.

Chapter 2: Literature Review

In this explorative, qualitative study, the researcher addressed the problem regarding the question of how personality traits of consumers perceive value as determined by perceived usefulness (PU) and perceived ease of use (PEOU) when considering online paid knowledge (OPK) products among consumers in the United States (Bahl et al., 2019; Fu et al., 2020; Jin & Xu, 2020; Jing et al., 2020; Su et al., 2019; Usakli, 2019). Exploring the phenomena of how different personality traits describe value provides an in-depth understanding of consumer perceptions of paid online courses. Chapter 2 begins with an overview of the technology acceptance model (TAM) as the theoretical framework. Then, to provide context, seminal research that underlies the identified problem and the purpose of this study is introduced.

A review of the evolution of TAM provides a background and a broad perspective of the origin of the theoretical framework research. The literature review examined the model's critics and other theories regarding behavior and technology. Existing and alternative frameworks are reviewed, including historical literature, concepts, and examples of previous studies. Other relevant technology theories not chosen for this study were also justified. The literature review examines TAM research in various settings, including business, healthcare, mobile, and marketing. The research also emphasizes the application of online shopping and perceived value through the TAM model.

Narrowing down online shopping to online learning began with background information regarding the history of online learning. Then, moving through the evolution of online learning provides a foundation of context for the current environment of the (OPK) market. This section includes an assessment of MOOCs (massive open online courses), the transition from free to paid, the (OPK) market, and the significance of digital entrepreneurs in the market.

Understanding the background of this phenomenon expands the TAM framework and supports the theory.

Subsequently, a discussion of the five-factor model (FFM) of personality traits and how it relates to the theoretical framework is reviewed. This section includes a brief history, a review of FFM use in consumer behavior research, and critiques regarding the application of this model. Bridging the TAM model and FFM application served as the guiding framework regarding OPK, PU, PEOU, and perceived value relevant to the current study. Finally, the researcher presents a summary to restate the key points and emphasize the importance of this study in terms of the gaps identified in the literature review.

For this literature review, the following databases were accessed: EBSCO, Science Direct, SpringerLink, JSTOR, EBSCOHost, Google Scholar, and Web of Science. In addition, the following keywords were delineated to access relevant literature: *TAM, FFM model, OPK, free to paid content, digital entrepreneurs, personality traits, TAM and FFM model, digital content industry, knowledge economy, PU, and PEOU.* Finally, to ensure relevant data in the assessment, a series of inclusion criteria were delineated, which included full-text literature and peer-reviewed assessments. The purpose of this criteria was to ensure that the collected literature was empirically evaluated and represented a full discussion of the research methods and outcomes.

Theoretical Framework Overview

The research used the technology acceptance model (TAM) framework and the five-factor model of personality (FFM) as antecedents to guide this qualitative case study. TAM presumes that if a particular technology is easy to use and useful, a person will perceive value and use it (Ajibade, 2018; Davis, 1989; Yu et al., 2005). TAM has been examined in many contexts, including but not limited to healthcare, banks, telecommunication, and manufacturing. Recently, Seibert et al. (2021) reviewed the current state of research on personality traits and the acceptance of technology. Seibert et al. (2021) further stated that many researchers use TAM to measure technology acceptance but further noted that the majority of research in this area was related to students and suggested that research expand to other social classes (Baki et al., 2021; Bruso et al., 2020; Seibert et al., 2021). FFM has been studied with TAM and has proven effective for explaining personalities in technology use (Bandera et al., 2020; Devaraj et al., 2008; Gvili et al., 2019; Harb & Alhayajneh, 2019; Marbach et al., 2016; Prasetya et al., 2015). The qualitative research methodology supports the chosen theoretical framework and allows for a more comprehensive understanding of the phenomenon, as called for by Usakli (2019). TAM and FFM are further examined in this literature review with relevance to the current research.

Summary of Seminal Research

Early researchers, such as Davis (1989), Devaraj et al. (2008), and Venkatesh (2003), began researching acceptance of technology among consumers, using models such as TAM, FFM, and UTAUT (unified theory of acceptance and use of technology) to explain the relationship with personality and technology (Chao, 2019; Seibert et al., 2021). As technology has progressed, research on consumer traits and attitudes toward online shopping has also progressed (Aldousari et al., 2016; Arora et al., 2018; Barnett et al., 2015; Bosnjak et al., 2007; Bucko et al., 2018; Chen, 2011; Fu et al., 2020; Wu & Ke, 2015). More specifically, several studies regarding technology and online learning were conducted (Abyaa et al., 2019; Altalhi, 2021; Bahl et al., 2018; Baki et al., 2021; Bawack et al., 2021; Cebi et al., 2022; Idrizi et al., 2021; Svendsen et al., 2013; Venkatesh et al., 2014).

There has been some initial research on the OPK market (Agarwal, 2015; Cai et al., 2020; Chen et al., 2021; Fang et al., 2021; Fu et al., 2020; Jin et al., 2020; Jing et al., 2020; Shi et al., 2018; Su et al., 2019; Liu et al., 2015; Yin et al., 2021; Zhu et al., 2019). For example, RuBell (2020) researched the monetization of online content by focusing on paywall solutions. In comparison, Zhang et al. (2020) used signaling effects to analyze determinants for online sales. Finally, Zhou et al. (2022) researched the purchase intention of online paid knowledge and found an overall lack of relevant literature in the knowledge payment industry. However, as this is a fast-developing market, consistency in definitions has added complexity to the study. Furthermore, different terms used for OPK research add to the confusion. A reference of terms used in research can be found in Appendix A to clarify and define the market.

This study extended the literature by Zhang (2020) and Zhou et al. (2022) in several ways. First, Zhou et al. (2022) used structural equation modeling (SEM) and a new stimulus-organism-response model to analyze Chinese respondents' data in the knowledge payment industry. Second, Zhou et al. (2022) studied perceived value based on environmental cues. This study adds to the body of literature by expanding the scope of perceived value among U.S. participants using personality traits as antecedents. Zhang et al. (2020) used signaling theory to determine sales of paid knowledge content focusing on one platform. Conversely, this study used TAM theory to address perceived value rather than sales determinants. As recommended, this research aimed to contribute to the body of literature and attempt to fill the gap of research on the topic by examining the phenomena with the in-depth perspective of qualitative research (Allan, 2020; Aspers & Corte, 2019; Usakli, 2019).

The Technology Acceptance Model (TAM)

The technology acceptance model (TAM) demonstrates how users adopt and use technology (Davis, 1989). The TAM model guides researchers in understanding that users, when presented with recent technology, are most likely to face a variety of factors that influence their ultimate decision to use the system (Chao, 2019; McElroy, 2007; Straub, 2009). Davis first developed the TAM theory to consider expanding the literature on the theory of reasoned action (TRA) and the theory of planned behavior (TPB) (Venkatesh, 2003). TAM grew upon TRA by considering the attitude measures: ease of use and usefulness (Alonso & Romero, 2017; Harari et al., 2018; Hoyte, 2019; Venkatesh, 2003). TRA and TPB are further discussed in this review's "Additional Theories" section.

The TAM theory is important to technological considerations in consumer-based research as it demonstrates how individuals perceive the use of the technology and how likely they are to use it (Alonso & Romero, 2017; Choudhury et al., 2020). Bagozzi (1992) considered this theory useful because advancing technologies are complex, and decision-makers have unpredictability regarding their perceptions of adopting recent technologies. The TAM model has three main factors (Davis, 1989; Straub, 2009; Venkatesh, 2003). These factors, which are essential to the current study, include perceived usefulness (PU), perceived ease of use (PEOU), and behavioral intention (BI) (Ajzen, 2020; Davis, 1989).

Davis first defined PU as the element in which an individual believes the system was helpful in their performance (Alarcon et al., 2018; Davis, 1989; Widiger & McCabe, 2020). PU is important in assessing technology acceptance and helps determine consumers' desires (Chintalapati & Daruri, 2017; Kumar et al., 2017). The next factor, PEOU, includes the individual's ability to use a particular technology with few difficulties (Bahaj et al., 2019;

Pookulangara et al., 2021; Wu & Ke, 2015). In the ever-changing landscape of technology, consumers deal with large amounts of information and seek resources that require low effort. Therefore, PU and PEOU have a significant impact on consumer satisfaction (Shah, 2016).

In the TAM model, behavioral intention is a factor that considers why consumers are more likely to use a specific technology (Alarcon et al., 2018; Ashraf et al., 2014; Davis, 1989; Hyatt et al., 2019; Molinillo, 2021; Munoz-Leiva et al., 2017; Sanchez-Prieto et al., 2017). The TAM model suggests that behavioral intention results from the consumer's PU, PEOU, and attitudes (Davis, 1989; Zhou et al., 2019). Davis (1986) explained behavior intention as being mediated by attitude in early versions of the model. Later versions of the TAM model eliminated the attitude construct as PU and PEOU were considered attitudes and perceptions.

Connecting Perceived Value With Behavioral Intention

Researchers have employed the consumer perceived value theory and TAM to create new models for considering perceived value. For example, Yu et al. (2005) employed the TAM model and customer perceived value to investigate users' acceptance behavior in mobile commerce. Analysis was conducted through interviews regarding perceived value factors and PEOU. The findings indicated that PEOU significantly impacts users' behavior, consumer innovativeness, and technology acceptance.

The consumer attitude, also described as perceived value, is the general impression that an individual gains from use and is considered a vital factor in behavioral intention (Gao, 2017; Gao, 2021; Hyatt et al., 2019; Li, 2017). Perceived value is a trade-off of sacrifices and benefits and is the difference between the consumer's perception and the opportunity cost of purchasing the product (Li et al., 2020; Marbach et al., 2016). For example, in a study on the impact of perceived value and behavior intention among parent-child runners in a marathon, the researcher found that the perceived value placed on the opportunity for parents to bond with their children ultimately influenced the behavioral intention of participating in the event (Li et al., 2021).

Perceived value involves interaction between the consumer and the subject or product (Holbrook, 2006; Hsiao, 2021). A consumer's intention to purchase knowledge products relies on knowledge received, as well as organization, selection, interpretation of knowledge, and the value they expect to receive (Hosta & Zabkar, 2021; Seibert et al., 2021; Su et al., 2017; Su et al., 2019). Online consumer engagement and aesthetic value are related to an easy-to-use layout and are directly related to perceived value (Ashraf et al., 2014; Bleier et al., 2019; Marbach et al., 2016; Marbach et al., 2019; RuBell et al., 2020). Attitude refers to the consumer's perception of the technology upon their first exposure (Biucky & Harandi, 2017; Zhou et al., 2019). For example, an extended model of TAM to study behavior intentions in telehealth found that improving ease of use and information quality improved the elderly's attitude regarding willingness to accept and adopt the technology (Zhou et al., 2019). In addition, research has shown that perceived value influences behavior intentions (Gao, 2021; Mohamad et al., 2021; Sanchez-Fernandez et al., 2007; Watjatrakul, 2020). Therefore, based on the relevance to behavior intention, consumer perceived value was addressed in this study (Ajzen, 2020; Shachak et al., 2019).

TAM Variations and Reliability in Research

The TAM framework has been used frequently across numerous studies and organizations during the past two decades (Svendsen et al., 2013). As a result, the TAM theory has been significantly researched regarding the examination's robustness and validity. For example, research from Lala (2014) examined the TAM model by focusing on how it evolved, its key applications, and criticisms of the theory. In particular, the author noted that the TAM model has been expanded in multiple variations and has been found to have adequate affective validity and reliability. Researchers have found the TAM's high reliability and adequate test-retest reliability a strong framework when researching technology. In addition, the model's simplicity allows the framework in various settings and is relatively straightforward for a researcher to reproduce the study (Lala, 2014; Mohamad et al., 2021).

Since researchers have used TAM in various settings, external and internal attributes have been used in combination with TAM (Devaraj et al., 2008). In addition, the model has expanded using different variables and antecedents based on several types of research (Baki et al., 2021; Changchit et al., 2019; Chintalapati & Daruri, 2017; Kumar et al., 2017; Mohamad, 2021). For example, the TAM 2 model used antecedents of perceived usefulness, such as job relevance and compatibility in the Toyota Astra Motor case study (Wahyuning et al., 2019). In addition, TAM 2 expanded TAM by contextualizing technology environments in employer-mandated systems (Lim, 2018). The TAM 3 model also expanded TAM by using variables (self-confidence, anxiety, facilitating conditions and pleasure) to explain the social influence of perceived ease of use, as in the study of Google Drive storage in e-learning (Baki et al., 2021; Lai, 2017; Setiyani et al., 2021; Wahyuning et al., 2019). Each factor in TAM is an essential consideration regarding technology usage and adoption (Ashraf et al., 2014; Davis, 1989; Hyatt et al., 2019; Xu et al., 2021). Subsequent research noted that the TAM theory is a reliable and proper test for exploring predicted validity regarding self-reported usage, attitudes towards use, and indicated validity for intent to use technology (Hindardjo, 2021; Lala, 2014; Mohamad et al., 2021).

Foundational Theories and Evolution of TAM

Acknowledging the theoretical history that underlies previous research in consumer behavior allows for context within the TAM Framework. Consumer behavior theory was first discussed in the 1940s to the 1950s and is a structure for studying how consumers decide, select and use specific goods and services offered by retailers (Hosta & Zabkar, 2021; Shin et al., 2018). During this time, marketing studies emerged from subsets of anthropology, ethnography, and sociological fields (Khan, 2020; Taufique & Vaithiananthan, 2018). Research from sociological and anthropological fields demonstrated that individuals behave in specific ways based on internal and external influences (Sirgy, 2018). As a result, the marketing field emerged, including explorations regarding consumer behavior and the impact on the selection and desire of goods and services (Shin et al., 2018). More recently, the Covid-19 pandemic has expanded consumer behavior theory and research (Chang, 2020; Chen et al., 2020; Rivers, 2021; Yin et al., 2021).

Two basic categories summarize consumer-based research: physiological and non-physiological. Psychological and physiological factors influence consumer-buying habits (Askadilla et al., 2017; Kachamas et al., 2019). For example, within physiological processes, individuals require basic needs, such as food, water, and sleep (Strommen-Bakhtiar, 2020). These underlying physiological needs are essential for specific purchasing patterns and behaviors (Gokhale et al., 2021). Additionally, non-physiological conditions such as self-actualization, self and personal growth, and buying items can help them fulfill these needs (Gokhale et al., 2021).

Contemporary research has greatly expanded the previous understanding of non-physiological consumer behavior (Han & Stoel, 2017; Yin et al., 2021). For example, researchers used consumer behavior theory to examine behavior through advanced methods, such as machine learning and neuroscience, which employed different technological platforms and tools to predict how consumers respond to specific platforms, goods, and services (Ghifarini et al., 2018). As a result, new behavior theories evolved with advancements in technology.

Additional Theories Related to Behavior and Technology

Theory of Reasoned Action (TRA) as a Precursor to TAM

From the foundation of consumer behavior research, new theories about technology emerged. The theory of reasoned action (TRA) was first developed in 1975 by Fishbein (Ajzen, 2012; Lai, 2017; Taherdoost, 2018). TRA is a theoretical framework for exploring individual relationships regarding attitudes and behaviors resulting from past beliefs (Otieno et al., 2016; Xiao, 2020). TRA has been popularized since the 1960s and 1970s due to extensive social psychological research and a renewed understanding of consumer behaviorism and its impact on purchasing intentions (Karnowski et al., 2018; Procter et al., 2019). More recently, researchers have employed the TRA framework to understand behavior patterns in utilizing technology (Otieno et al., 2016; Procter et al., 2019). For example, Karnowski et al. (2018) used TRA to analyze news-sharing behavior but suggested limitations due to the omission of attitudes and intentions. TAM is a simplified version of TRA, as it excludes beliefs about other people's opinions (Ajzen, 2020). This study's purpose and research questions are not based on past beliefs and subjective norms but on personality traits. Therefore, they were not considered appropriate in the current study.

Theory of Planned Behavior (TPB) as a Precursor to TAM

The theory of planned behavior (TPB) is also a popular model in behavior-based marketing research and consists of six constructs: attitudes, behavioral intention, subjective norms, social norms, perceived power, and perceived behavioral control (Ajzen, 2020; Davis,

1989; Han & Stoel, 2017; Yuriev et al., 2020). TPB, introduced in the 1980s, is an extension of TRA to understand how individuals are likely to engage in behavior during specific times and periods and acknowledge both the constructs of motivation and ability (Ajzen, 2020; Gao et al., 2017; Yuriev et al., 2020). However, TPB has primarily been used to understand behavioral intentions regarding tangible products such as smoking, drinking, health services, and substance abuse (Sussman & Gifford, 2019; Yuriev et al., 2020). For example, Scott et al. (2019) used the TPB model to research technology adoption in the gambling industry.

Behavioral intention in TPB is the individual's ability to control themselves in the face of a specific desire or product, such as smoking or drinking (Hamilton et al., 2020; Miller, 2017). For example, some individuals may find drinking in public is socially unlikable or goes against their norms (Savari & Gharechaee, 2020; Verma & Chandra, 2018). Subjective norms refer to individuals' beliefs regarding the approval or disapproval of engaging in these specific events or products (Carfora et al., 2019; Hamilton et al., 2020). Jain et al. (2017) found that subjective norms were the most crucial factor in purchasing luxury fashion goods. Finally, perceived power is the influence of the individual to control themselves and their behavior (Savari & Gharechaee, 2020; Verma & Chandra, 2018).

Both TRA and TPB examine behavioral intention, attitude, and subjective norms. The TPB theory is important for marking research and was adapted along with TRA to develop TAM. However, TPB is not best suited for this study as it suggests that these are the only factors needed to establish an accurate behavior prediction and is used at a general level, whereas TAM is content-specific (Ajzen, 2020; Gao et al., 2017; Sussman & Gifford, 2019). Instead, the desire to examine personality factors concerning technology and TAM contributed to this theoretical framework using perceived value (as evidenced by behavioral intention) while also considering the mediators of PU of use and PEOU.

Unified Theory of Acceptance and Use of Technology (UTAUT)

The TAM theory has also been expanded to include the unified theory of acceptance and use of technology (Lai, 2017; Lala, 2014). The unified theory of acceptance and use of technology (UTAUT) was a theory developed by Venkatesh et al. (2003). The abovementioned theories predict behavioral intention by adding additional antecedents (Altalhi, 2021; Shachak et al., 2019; Venkatesh, 2003). UTAUT explains intentions in technology innovation and user behavior. In addition, it explores e-commerce, trust, and perceived risk (Otieno et al., 2016). This model effectively evaluates the latest technologies using effort expectancy, performance expectancy, social influence, and facilitating conditions (Harb & Alhayajneh, 2019; Venkatesh et al., 2003). Sinha et al. (2019) suggested that this theory was essential in studying online education. Wrycza et al. (2017) used an adapted version to review the acceptance of software tools in academic education.

Research has studied paying behavior of online courses using UTAUT and included variables such as perceived interaction, trust, and cost as well as content quality but did not address how different consumers' personalities responded to the antecedents (Mendoza et al., 2017; Yu et al., 2021). However, critics of this theory cite clarity difficulty due to using too many variables (Lai, 2017). As the purpose of the study was not to consider e-commerce, trust, and risk, the researcher did not use UTAUT but instead used the TAM framework. While UTAUT builds on TAM, TAM focuses more on attitudes and perceptions, including PU and PEOU, and fits this study's construct more appropriately (Mendoza et al., 2017; Shachak et al., 2019).

Criticism of TAM

While the TAM model is the most used framework when researching technology

adoption and acceptance, it has some criticisms and limitations (Ajibade, 2018; Lai, 2017; Lim,

2018; Venkatesh, 2003). For example, critics argue that TAM does not consider variables such

as personality traits or social norms, which can often motivate behavior intention (Ajibade, 2018;

Lai, 2017; Lala, 2014). Another criticism of the TAM model is that it reduces the structure to

three factors and leaves out the concept of actual use as well as the predictive powers of

technology (Lim, 2018). Furthermore, in the development of the UTAUT model, Venkatesh

(2003) stated that user experience was not included in TAM, thus, leaving out an important

consideration in studying technology acceptance. Additionally, TAM is criticized as not

applicable for business entities but focuses on individual beliefs, perceptions, and usage

intentions (Shachak, 2019). More recently, TAM has been criticized for its relevance in

technology adoption, citing that today's consumers have better technological knowledge and

education, and the relevance of the model is no longer relevant (Lim, 2018).

TAM Studied in Various Settings

TAM Researched on the Internet of Things (IoT)

TAM is a framework for exploring technologies like the Internet of Things (Al-Abdullatif

et al., 2022; Almazroi, 2022). These opportunities benefit business models and migrate away

from traditional projects and service-based acquisition, a foundational element of many service

industries. For example, Paiola and Gebauer (2020) focused on the influence of technology of

things and technological products in changing business models and financial streams. The

authors noted that digital service station has often been improved strategically to companies' use of technology and ability to understand perceived ease of use and the attractiveness of the

technology by the consumer.

TAM Researched in Banking

Recently, the banking industry has evolved to include mobile banking. The TAM model

is a helpful framework for this industry (Juliani et al., 2021; Kumar et al., 2017; Mori, 2020).

Research using TAM in mobile banking found a positive effect on intention directly related to

PU and PEOU (Juliani et al., 2021; Kumar et al., 2017; Munoz-Leiva et al., 2017). Kumar et al.

(2017) stated that m-commerce is an innovation with value-added applications. In further

support, Munoz-Leiva et al. (2017) found that interaction and engagement are associated with

perceived value. However, the relationship between intention to use and perceived risk was

weak.

TAM Researched in the Service Industry

Similarly, Mohamad et al. (2021) examined how mobile technological adaption has

influenced customers' intentions through the TAM model. This author's explanation further

explained how the TAM model is used in consumer-based research. According to these authors,

survey data included 386 travelers likely to book hotel rooms through their smartphones. The

data was analyzed following a structural modeling equation to address PU, PEOU, perceived

enjoyment, and perceived price value regarding consumers' behavioral intention toward mobile

hotel booking technology. The findings indicated that TAM is useful for consumer-based

research and can be extended for predicting how individuals will use recent technology,

specifically within the service industry. As a result, researchers tend to extend the TAM model or

add external attributes (Mohamad et al., 2021). However, the authors noted a further need for extended research regarding personality and consumer-based behavior factors that influence digital services, a new and influential element of business models.

TAM Researched in Social Media

Social media is a growing area in technology (Al-Qaysi et al., 2022). As a result, technological theories expanded, such as diffusion of innovation, TRA, TPB, and TAM (Arora & Aggarwal, 2018; Chopdar et al., 2018). In addition, TAM explains decision processes and internal and external variables influenced by social media (Izogo & Jayawardhena, 2018; Simanjuntak, 2019). Research using the TAM framework demonstrates PU and PEOU in social media (Alduaij, 2019; Al-Qaysi et al., 2020; Hyun et al., 2022). Further, we have seen the growth of online shopping due to social media influencers with celebrities and the public aligning with specific brands (Wang & Lee, 2021). Influencers shifted consumers to be motivated and engaged with the product they previously were unlikely to purchase (Dhanesh & Duther, 2019; Simanjuntak, 2019).

TAM and Online Shopping

Online shopping grew in popularity as individuals quickly responded to marketing by purchasing a computer for work, socialization, personal purposes, and Internet use (Pappas et al., 2017). As early as the 1960s and 1970s, researchers noted that there would be an increased examination of Internet consumer behavior due to recent technologies, such as the Internet and the computer (Su et al., 2017; Wang & Qu, 2017). Online shopping led to a new field in consumer behavior focused on Internet consumer behavior and technology (Su et al., 2017; Wang & Qu, 2017). Research in online shopping has employed TAM, including buying choices buying intention, and cultural contexts (Aldousari et al., 2016; Changchit et al., 2019; Ha et al., 2021). There are two specific considerations in online shopping: consumer value in purchasing and product value (Izogo & Jayawardhena, 2018). The experience gained in online shopping must be engaging and increase shopper satisfaction compared to a physical store when considering the value in purchasing (Su et al., 2017; Wang & Qu, 2017; Zhao et al., 2021). Product value is usually similar in online and offline shopping (Wang & Qu, 2017).

In online shopping, individuals are satisfied based on how easily they navigate the website and obtain their desired needs (Chakraborty & Bhat, 2018). For example, Bahari et al. (2018) found that website design quality positively affected PU and PEOU. Also, elements such as price, value, and time commitment are important for individuals in online shopping (Ijaz & Rhee, 2018). As a result, online shopping and behavior research expanded to understand how purchase decisions are variable based on consumer behavior (Ali, 2020; Chakraborty & Bhat, 2018). Additionally, as the Internet and technology advanced, multiple platforms in which individuals could engage with online shopping were created (Simanjuntak, 2019). For example, tools now include iPads, smartphones, and computers (Ali, 2020). Online shopping is planned, spontaneous, or impulsive among consumers (Ijaz & Rhee, 2018). Either way, individuals are easily interconnected with online shopping platforms in a way previously unseen before the advent of technology and the Internet, demonstrating technology acceptance and support for the TAM framework in this study (Izogo & Jayawardhena, 2018; Min et al., 2019).

TAM Researched in Knowledge Sharing

Yu et al. (2005) researched TAM from the perspective of voluntary consumer sharing of e-service knowledge within an online community. The authors noted that the TAM model might contribute to a further understanding of personal attributes, including consumer innovativeness and subjective knowledge. For their assessment, the authors employed perceived ease of use and usefulness in predicting consumer volunteering knowledge in the context of an online community. Data was analyzed and collected from 364 airline travelers recruited from an online

traveling community within China. The findings indicate that personal factors are strong drivers

for sharing services within e-service platforms. Further, creating common knowledge within

online communities may improve e-firm service strategies by focusing on these individual

factors. Other recent studies of knowledge sharing using the TAM framework demonstrate PU

and PEOU (Al-Emran et al., 2021; Pang et al., 2020; Rashid et al., 2021). Data such as these

studies further demonstrate the importance of including TAM within consumer-based market

research and considering personal behavioral factors (Zamani et al., 2021).

TAM in Online Learning

Extensive research on TAM in online learning further demonstrates justification of the

framework for this study (Arifianto & Izzudin, 2021; Hernandez, 2021; Mustafa et al., 2021);

Sriwardiningsih, E., 2021; Dai et al., 2021). An example of testing applications of the TAM

model in online learning includes Mohammadi's (2015) analysis of perspectives to determine

how consumers perceive quality features, PU and PEOU, on users' intention and satisfaction,

and mediating variables in e-learning. Data was gathered through a consumer survey and

analyzed using structural equation modeling. The findings indicated that intention and user

satisfaction positively affect e-learning services and that mediating factors, such as system

quality and information quality, are primary drivers of users' intention and satisfaction with e-

learning software.

Tan (2019) extended these findings by focusing on college students learning attitudes and

employee tutoring websites. The authors employed college students' assessment of self-paced

business English e-learning websites to assess their adaption and perceived ease of use. The

findings used linear regression analysis and indicated that, with the TAM model, business

English e-learning websites were more likely to gain customer loyalty if they could enhance the quality of the sites and ensure support and ease of use. Examples such as this demonstrate how the TAM model determines a consumer's ability and likelihood to use technology and improve current business models (Svendsen et al., 2013; Tan, 2019).

Five-Factor Model (FFM) of Personality

This research included the five-factor model (FFM) as a construct within the TAM framework discussed in the previous section. The FFM was developed to consider individual personalities and assess specific treatment dimensions (Caprara et al., 1993; Drislane et al., 2018; McCrae & Costa, 2008; McCrae, 2009). In personality studies, the FFM is the most widely used theory used to categorize and define personality models in research (Barnett et al., 2015; Boyle, 2008; Chung et al., 2018; Devaraj et al., 2008; McCrae & Costa, 2008). Personality traits show minor changes throughout a person's life and demonstrate their thought patterns, emotion, and behavior and are, therefore, a reliable construct in research (Bahcekapili & Karaman, 2020).

The FFM is sometimes called the "big five" or "big five inventory" (Bruso et al., 2020; Caprara, 1993; McCrae, 2009). The big five questionnaire is an instrument used to measure personality traits and includes five dimensions of personality: extraversion, agreeableness, conscientiousness, neuroticism, and openness to experience (Bagby & Widiger, 2018; Caprara et al., 1993; Chehreh et al., 2017; Gvili et al., 2019; McCrae, 2009; Souri et al., 2018). Personality psychologists often find that the big five assessment is appropriate for capturing visual differences as well as specific and often variable personality traits (Caprara, 1993; Chen, 2011; Kajonius & Giolla, 2017).

Extraversion (Outgoing/Energetic vs. Solitary/Reserved)

The personality type of extraversion in the FFM includes either outgoing, energetic or solitary, and reserved individuals. Highly extroverted individuals are often considered assertive and sociable compared to quiet and reserved individuals. Outgoing and energetic individuals are often referred to as extroverts (Chehreh et al., 2017; Souri et al., 2018; Smith et al., 2019). In contrast, solitary and reserved individuals are referred to as introverts (Smith et al., 2019). Introverts are more likely to be reserved, enjoy reduced social stimulation, and enjoy spending time alone (Toschi et al., 2018). However, these characteristics do not mean they are antisocial or avoid people, but rather gain stimulation from spending time with themselves and engaging in enjoyable activities at home (Smith et al., 2019; Souri et al., 2018). Conversely, extroverts are more likely to gain social stimulation from socializing with others and enjoy spending most of their time with individuals who share similar likes and interests (Toschi et al., 2018).

Agreeableness (Friendly/Compassionate vs. Critical/Rational)

Agreeableness includes either friendly and compassionate individuals or critical and rational individuals (Sleep et al., 2021). Individuals that are friendly and compassionate are more likely to be concerned with the welfare of others, be kind and generous, as well as willing to compromise their own interests to meet the need of their friends, families, and societal purposes, such as climate change and sustainability (Etkin et al., 2020; Nezlek & Forestell, 2019). Conversely, critical and rational individuals are more likely to be concerned with their own needs than others (Widiger & McCabe, 2020). Individuals who are disagreeable are more likely to extend their well-being to themselves or close circuits (Widiger & McCabe, 2020). Further, disagreeable individuals are more likely to be skeptical, often unfriendly, and generally uncooperative (Etkin et al., 2020).

Openness to Experience (Inventive/Curious vs. Consistent/Cautious)

The personality trait of openness to experience includes either inventive and curious or consistent and cautious individuals (Etkin et al., 2020). Individuals open to experience are often inquisitive and interested in art and education (Caprara, 1993; Nezlek & Forestell, 2019; Smith et al.). In some cases, openness to experience is referred to as intellect. Individuals open to experiences are more likely to engage in unconventional activities and hold unconventional beliefs (Sleep et al., 2021). Openness to experience can also include engaging in risky behaviors (Toschi et al., 2018). Individuals that are not open to experience are more consistent and cautious (Etkin et al., 2020). For this purpose, they are more interested in self-actualization and gaining self-satisfaction through pragmatic and data-driven decisions (Widiger & McCabe, 2020).

Conscientiousness (Efficient/Organized vs. Extravagant/Careless)

Conscientious individuals are either efficient and organized or extravagant and careless (Kajonius & Johnson, 2018; Wehner et al., 2021). Individuals who are efficient and organized are more likely to make careful data-driven decisions and focus on factors that ensure effective work, social, and personal outcomes (Wehner et al., 2021). Conversely, individuals who are not conscientious are more likely to be extravagant and careless individuals who may spend money on items that fulfill personal wants and desires and engage in compulsive buying behaviors (Chehreh et al., 2017; Souri et al., 2018).

Neuroticism (Sensitive/Nervous vs. Resilient/Confident)

The personality trait of neuroticism includes either sensitive and nervous individuals or resilient and confident individuals (Owens et al., 2019). Neurotic individuals are often more prone to negative emotions, such as anxiety, depression, and irritation, than emotionally resilient individuals (Barr, 2018; Caprara, 1993; Liu et al., 2021). In addition, this personality trait is often linked to lacking emotional stability (Abood et al., 2019; Caprara, 1993; Riccelli et al., 2017). On the other hand, some individuals that are neurotic are resilient and confident and experience high coping strategies for stress (Abood et al., 2019). Individuals' ability to cope with neuroticism is linked to their behavioral patterns and purchasing and decision-making processes (Feist, 2019; Lui et al., 2020).

FFM Used in Consumer Behavior Research

FFM Research in Healthcare

Healthcare is an area studied with personality traits (Barr, 2018; He & He., 2021; Lee, 2013). For example, Lee (2013) additionally conducted a study regarding personality traits in Taiwan with a specific focus on health care tourism products. The authors addressed health knowledge, product attributes, purchasing intent, and personality traits. The findings indicated that consumers' health knowledge, involvement, product attributes, and personality traits impact their intent to purchase. Additionally, He and He (2021) researched pilots' personality traits and mental health, and Barr (2018) analyzed work stress among nurses. Research, such as the findings in this section, illustrates that consideration of personality factors is a critical consideration that dominates contemporary consumer-based research.

FFM Research in Business

Previous assessments have also focused on the personality factors impacting small and medium exporting organizations (Anwar, M. & Claub, T., 2021; Kimixay & Liu, 2018; Matarazzo et al., 2021; Runst, P. & Thoma, J., 2021). For example, the personality traits of digital entrepreneurs and managers of small and medium organizations affect their experiences and actions (Bandera et al., 2020; Montenegro, 2020; Runst, P. & Thoma, J., 2021). Montenegro (2020) focused on Colombia, where many small businesses have become influential international organizations. The qualitative case study data demonstrated that personality factors are key to the likelihood of managers using the Internet. In particular, personality factors impact managers' skills and the possibility of being innovative and learning innovative marketing strategies based on online or Internet-based tools. Digital transformation and network structures analyzed with personality traits in small to medium enterprises is another area of research (Li et al., 2017; Matarazzo et al., 2021; Selden & Goodie, 2018). Lane (1993) similarly suggested a new consideration of managing customer-based brand equity through a specific focus on consumers' perceptions and personality traits. Lane (1993) argued that customer-based brand equity is most important for considering how individuals are loyal to a brand and are likely to purchase and stay within the company. Keller and Lehmann (2006) also recommended similar recommendations to Lane (1993). They argued that brands and branding processes must prioritize brand equity to understand the consumer base and mindset.

FFM Research in Smartphones

Researchers have focused on personality traits in various scenarios of technology advancement. For example, Maier et al. (2020) and Gao et al. (2022) studied personality traits and smartphone usage. In addition, Maier (2020) conducted a qualitative study of personality traits of smartphone use while driving. Further, Gao et al. (2021) wrote a meta-analytic review of the problematic use of mobile phones in different personality traits, while Chopdar et al. (2018) analyzed mobile shopping apps and perceived risk. Each of these studies connected personality traits to consumer usage of smartphones indicating that personality traits affect technology usage.

FFM Research in Technostress

Pflugner et al. (2020) examined personality profiles regarding user risk of technostress. The author gathered data through a questionnaire distributed to 221 users across different organizations. The findings in the qualitative comparative analysis indicated that personality traits uniquely impact high techno stressors. Similarly, Cai et al. (2018) studied personality traits and technology stress and found correlations between personality traits and technology stress using wearable devices. These findings illustrate that it is important to consider personality factors driving consumers away from the platform in developing an online shopping market. However, these also focused upon explorations that excluded the TAM and FFM model, which the current study addresses.

FFM Research in Online Shopping

Researchers also demonstrate the importance of considering personality characteristics when assessing online shopping (Ngah et al., 2022; Roos & Kazemi, 2022; Wu et al., 2018). For example, Fernandes et al. (2021) examined the online susceptibility scale, which focused on individuals' likelihood of purchasing in an online environment by considering personality factors. The authors also conducted a factor analysis to assess online information sources' impact on shopper buying decisions. The findings indicate that individuals are more susceptible to online shopping based on decision-making and personal factors.

Huang et al. (2017) also studied personality in online purchases. The authors examined social commerce regarding usability and design factors, such as usability, function ability, and social ability within the five stages of the decision-making process. The authors identified that social commerce design affects all five decision-making stages. In particular, individuals are more likely to use the software if they feel it is applicable and usable for their specific wants and needs.

Otero-Lopez et al. (2021) provided an exploration focused on the big five personality traits, coping strategies, and compulsive buying among Spanish university students. The sample included 1093 participants who classified themselves as compulsive online shoppers for the assessment. Surveys included their big five personality tests, gender, and age. The findings indicated that gender and neuroticism impacted the risk of compulsive shopping. Conversely, the traits of problem-solving, cognitive restructuring, and the conscientious dimension of the big five reduced compulsive shopping and improved coping skills. According to these authors, the findings are important as they illustrate the impact of personality traits when considering online shopping experiences, which hold important implications for market purchase buying research.

FFM Research in Online Learning

The role of personality traits in relevance to online learning is continually expanding in literature (Abe, 2020; Bruso et al., 2020). According to Calmbach et al. (2014), personality traits play a significant role in a person's preference for learning tools. In addition, Watjatrakul (2020) found that personality traits can moderate the perceived value and intention to study an online course.

Lai et al. (2019) applied a similar assessment focusing on students' online learning behavior and personality identification. The authors focused on data drawn from 662 senior high school students enrolled in online learning programs for the assessment. The findings indicated that students' personality was positively associated with their online learning behavior, thus, indicating that personality impacts the usability and the behavior of the consumer. Additionally,

Bidjerano, 2007 Bruso et al., 2020 conducted an examination of personality traits analyzing self-regulation in online learning.

More recently, personality traits and self-efficacy with external factors like the coronavirus pandemic indicated direct effects of personality traits in the Moodle learning management system and other online learning platforms (Rivers, 2021; Yu, 2021). Similarly, research on medical students' personality traits and engagement levels during the pandemic found that engagement levels were higher in the classroom than online learning (Toraman, 2021). Furthermore, Hong et al. (2021) also researched personality traits in online learning during the Covid-19 Pandemic and found that extraversion and neuroticism can predict performance anxiety. Finally, similar to this study, Ha et al. (2021) employed the FFM to consider factors of Vietnamese consumers' online shopping intention by focusing on the TAM and the TPB models. The authors examined data from 423 questionnaires using exploratory factor analysis and multiple regression assessment. According to the authors, PU, PEOU, attitude, subjective norm, and trust positively impacted consumers' online shopping intention.

FFM Research in Usability

Kortum and Oswald (2018) investigated the impact of personality on subjective usability assessment. The author gathered data from 268 users across twenty assorted products and work, school, and life-related technological domains for further research. The researchers examined personality traits in terms of the usability of the products. The findings indicated that openness to experience and agreeability among personality traits were most likely to influence a positive relationship regarding technology usability.

Researchers have also examined how expanding the facilitators' understanding of personality factors can improve the demographic understanding of developing economies. Sinha and Bagarukayo (2019) noted that the development of communication technologies had focused more closely on personality in terms of considering consumers and markets available for developing economies. The authors argue that there is a need to understand personality in terms of consumer likelihood to use specific tools and technologies. Burnett and Ditsikas (2006) also urged further understanding of personality as a criterion when considering usability. The findings indicated that extroverts were 40% more likely to use the platform when compared to introverts. Findings such as these further illustrate the importance of considering personality in terms of usability and online shopping-based products.

Critiques of the FFM

Block (1995) provided an opposing view of the FFM, citing that the model's constructs are not scientifically sufficient. Additionally, McCrae and Sutin (2007) reviewed FFM to consider unresolved questions and found that variable cultures can affect the results. Previous researchers also centered closely around the specific English semantics employed within the survey to delineate broad characteristics and personality traits. Boyle (2008) reviewed the FFM model. According to the author, the FFM relies on 35 clusters of trait syndromes, reducing 4000 English trait descriptors of personality. Boyle (2008) noted that while the personality dimensions can be useful, there are limitations concerning methodological applications of the sizes and distinctions between constructs labeled based on specific English words (Owens et al., 2019; Toschi et al., 2018; Widiger & Crego, 2019).

Critiques of the FFM have also centered on the importance of considering personality in particular (Alonso & Romero, 2017; Alonso & Romero, 2020; Harari et al., 2018; Usakli, 2019; Wakabayashi, 2020; Widiger & Crego, 2019). Devaraj et al. (2008) noted that while personality may be an important factor, it also requires further understanding regarding how personality impacts user attitudes and beliefs.

However, research using the FFM has been effectively employed in multiple empirical settings across the past quarter-century (Du et al., 2021; Smith et al., 2019). Further, McCrae (2009) noted that previous researchers have demonstrated that the model effectively provides an overall understanding of personality traits and characteristics. Thus, FFM is valid for considering consumer behavior in marketing-based strategies (Alonso & Romero, 2017; Harari et al., 2018; Hoyte, 2019).

Five-Factor Model (FFM) of Personality Traits in This Study

The "big five inventory" questionnaire used to establish the five factors of personality in the FFM is considered more reliable than in-person interviews (Bahcekapili et al., 2020; Barnett et al., 2015; Bawack et al., 2021; Usakli, 2019). In particular, interviews are more likely to introduce personal bias (Caprara, 1993; Condon, 2017; Daljeet et al., 2017). For example, an individual is likely to demonstrate their perceptions of their personality in an interview rather than an accurate quantitative perception of personality dimensions (Bagby & Widiger, 2018; Smith et al., 2019). Further, the FFM is an important assessment in providing a dimension of personality traits directly applicable to market-based research (Abyaa et al., 2019; Harris & Rouse, 2014). FFM has been validated to consider consumer behavior in marketing-based strategies (Alonso & Romero, 2017; Harari et al., 2018; Hoyte, 2019).

TAM Studied With FFM

It is essential to establish previous research on the FFM and TAM model together while also providing context for the application in the current study. Researchers have examined how individuals accept and use a specific technology using the TAM framework (Biucky & Harandi,

2017; Zhou et al., 2019). In recent consumer-based research, researchers have focused closely on the relationship between personality types and the impact of technology management systems (Barnett et al., 2015; Harb & Alhayajaneh, 2019; Prasetya et al., 2015). Additionally, Devaraj et al. (2008) gathered data from 180 users of collaborative technology. The authors found that FFM personality dimensions predict users' attitudes and beliefs. Finally, Svendsen et al. (2013) and Harb and Alhayajaneh (2019) researched the structure of the TAM model by assessing individual variables and relationships between personality and the TAM constructs. The authors noted that personality could influence behavior intention and indicated a need to extend the understanding of personalities' relationship with the TAM model in consumer behavior market research.

TAM and FFM in Stock Market and Social Media

Harb and Alhayajneh (2019) analyzed the assessment of TAM with a focus on the intention to use business intelligence tools when making decision-making processes. The authors found that FFM and TAM combined to improve the understanding of personality and purchasing intent. Similarly, Sussman (2020) used age as a moderator in PU and PEOU in the stock market. The authors specifically researched a quantitative non-experimental correlation study to examine the adoption of social media-based stock market movement for stock market investors (Sussman, 2020). The findings indicated that the significant moderators were PU and PEOU when predicted by age.

TAM and FFM in Internet Usage

Personality traits can impact factors of technology usage (Rivers, 2021; Roos & Kazemi, 2021; Tsao, 2013). McElroy et al. (2007) analyzed dispositional factors in terms of Internet usage by focusing on personality and cognitive styles using measures of Internet usage. The authors found that personality and cognitive style were variables as well as an antecedent towards use. In particular, using the FFM or "big five personality inventory" can improve market research base understanding of Internet usage and the predictive capabilities of consumer use and perceived ease of use using the TAM framework. Further, Tsao (2013) found that using personality traits as antecedents can modulate Internet usage into categories.

TAM and FFM in Software and Classroom Technology

The FFM framework has also been used to examine other operators that impact our ability, such as goals, actions, plans, or functions (Abedini, 2020; Baruth & Cohen, 2022; Yildiz, 2022). Researchers also applied FFM and TAM to analyze personality subsets of consumer behavior in the acceptance and outcome of a particular technology or consumer-based platform with the teacher's personality as a moderator (Vlachogianni et al., 2020). Further, Yildiz (2022) supported this analysis by researching personality traits in a flipped classroom. These findings demonstrate that the FFM can be beneficial for explaining the application of consumer-based value for specific technology consumer programs (Bouchet & Sansonnet, 2013; Rivers, 2021). Similarly, Barnett et al. (2015) also employed FFM to predict individuals' technology acceptance based on classroom technology use and perceived and actual use.

TAM and FFM in Learning Languages Online

Mirzaee (2016) examined learning perception based on college students' personality characteristics. For the analysis, the author gathered quantitative data from the personality questionnaire and added a modified web-based learning attitude and perception questionnaire. Interviews were also conducted to gain further qualitative understanding of college students' personality factor's impact on a language online. The findings indicated that the personality factors, extroverts and introverts, could create significant differences in learning perceptions. Chen et al. (2021) corroborated these findings by conducting a quantitative synthesis to analyze the relationships between personality traits and learning a second or foreign language. Similarly, for this study, the big five questionnaire was used to identify the personality traits as part of the demographic information.

TAM and FFM in Video Conferencing

The FFM model has been used more recently with the TAM model to interpret consumer's personality and behavioral characteristics in video conferencing technology (Rivers, 2021; Weiser et al., 2018). For example, Fondo et al. (2018) supported these results by analyzing foreign languages in videoconferencing. In addition, Lakhal and Khechine (2017) examined the TAM and the FFM model by examining how personality variables may impact acceptance in education settings. For the assessment, the authors gathered data from 413 individuals exposed to video conferencing technology in higher education. In addition, the authors examined social influence, performance expectancy, and facilitating conditions in terms of behavioral intentions. The findings indicated that neuroticism significantly affected performance expectancy, effort expectancy, and facilitating conditions.

TAM and FFM in Virtual Reality Shopping

Lixandroiu et al. (2021) analyzed the effects of personality traits regarding virtual reality online shopping in TAM. The authors reviewed the effects of personality traits and attitudes toward the Internet for the assessment within two electronic commerce forms. The findings indicated that buying intention and online shopping are significantly impacted by personality traits. In particular, neuroticism and openness to experiences are positively associated with individuals' willingness to buy in an online setting (McElroy et al., 2007; Mirzaee, 2016; Montenegro, 2020). Further, agreeableness positively impacted the expert effort expectancy and conscientiousness (Lixandroiu et al., 2021). Together, these researchers illustrate the effectiveness of the implication of the FFM in the TAM model in consumer behavior, personality, and usefulness factors.

TAM and FFM With Perceived Value Construct

Multiple factors underpin the key constructs of perceived value (Munoz-Leiva et al., 2017; Sanchez-Prieto et al., 2017). Marbach et al. (2016) examined the use of personality in customer perceived value in online engagement programs. The authors conducted 28 semi-structured interviews with social brand communities for the exploration. Their study aimed to consider engagement among personality traits. The findings indicated that personality traits are a critical factor influencing customer perceived value. Furthermore, the research illustrates that the focused words "brand equity" and "promotion" have been further enhanced by understanding personality traits through a combination of the FFM and TAM models (Keller & Lehmann, 2006; Mowen, 2000). Thus, indicating that when considering consumer behavior purchases, intentions, and attitudes, it is important to consider FFM as an assessment of personality traits (Marbach et al., 2016; McElroy et al., 2007).

Finally, the findings in the literature review demonstrate that FFM and TAM models are significantly valuable for future studies exploring how personality impacts the PU and PEOU in the acceptance of technological models (Bahl et al., 2019, Fu et al., 2020; Jin et al., 2020; Jing et al., 2020; Seibert et al., 2021; Su et al., 2019). Furthermore, they demonstrate that TAM is a continuing and valuable model to support the exploration of predictive analytics in technology. These findings demonstrate that regardless of the consumer-based exploration, personality factors may have individual and unique impacts on the perceived usefulness and the likelihood of engaging with a specific technology (Harb & Alhayajneh, 2019; McElroy et al., 2007; Mirzaee, 2016; Montenegro, 2020; Prasetya et al., 2015; Seibert et al., 2021; Zhou et al., 2007). Thus, reinforcing the study's methodology and design, FFM and TAM consider perceived value within market-based behavior processes.

Development of Online Learning Relevant to Current Study

The development and evolution of online learning is a broad demonstration of the TAM theory. For example, online learning is a new way of delivering courses, and TAM is an excellent model to explain how students perceive usefulness and ease of use (Lee, 2002). In this section, the researcher provides a basis for the study and use of the TAM model by exploring the history and background of online learning development and previous online learning examples related to the current study. A literature review on online learning development provides a foundation for the current study and supports TAM as the theoretical framework (Mustafa & Garcia., 2021). The literature review of online learning further supports the current study's research by demonstrating that consumer personality traits are important for Internet usage and online learning (Devaraj et al., 2008; Hepworth, 2007; Roos & Kazemi, 2021; Watjatrakul, 2020).

According to Regele (2020), literature on learning products developed by for-profit businesses is scarce. In the first section, MOOCs are reviewed. A discussion regarding free to paid-based e-learning commerce is also provided. Further, the researcher expands upon free to paid resources with a focus on digital entrepreneurs entering the market, which significantly changed e-learning procedures and the understanding of how to meet OPK based on consumer needs (Dhawan, 2020; Singh & Thurman, 2019). Previous research indicates that the advancements in online learning grew from pedagogy in education toward profit-based information products, including webinars, conferences, courses, and skills certifications (Regele, 2020; Reyna et al., 2020). Therefore, there is a need to understand further how the transition from free to paid content impacted consumer behavior theories as well as the benefits for the consumer and the organization (Lambrecht, 2017; Regele, 2020; Ye et al., 2021; Zhang et al., 2020).

There have been significant changes in how individuals gain knowledge. The rise of the Internet, in particular, has improved our understanding of how we can meet the needs of consumers and how individuals acquire knowledge through an online learning format (Mohammadi, 2015; Dhawan, 2020; Singh & Thurman, 2019). However, the current literature regarding e-learning illustrates a need to focus further on understanding and exploring modeling techniques that consider consumer variables, such as personality (Abyaa et al., 2019). The current study provides a funnel discussion within the TAM construct that initiates an understanding of online learning and the transition from free to paid learning and considers the importance of personality-based factors in terms of PU and PEOU. However, to provide a fundamental basis for this topic, the following section focuses on the first form of free online learning: MOOCs.

Massive Open Online Courses (MOOCs) Studied With TAM: A Predecessor to OPK

Massive open online courses (MOOCs) are an early form of the knowledge economy and are free online courses available for any individual to enroll. These programs provide an affordable and flexible way to gain online knowledge (Barger, 2020; Salikhova et al., 2020; Wang et al., 2019; Zykov, 2016). There are varying MOOCs to choose from, such as career development, college preparation, supplemental learning, e-learning, and training (Ceron et al., 2020; Cunha et al., 2020; Merriam & Baumgartner, 2020; Plewnia, 2018). There are currently over six thousand courses available, spanning business, engineering, humanities, and data science (Altalhi, 2021; Liyanagunawardena et al., 2015; Zhang et al., 2020; Zhu et al., 2020).

Additionally, Alyoussef (2021) utilized TAM theory to assess the sustainability of MOOCs. Findings suggested that using MOOCs is a sustainable way to influence student academic performance and that the PU of the MOOC system leads to increased usage (Lee, 2002). Other studies on MOOCs using the TAM theory include Hernandez et al. (2021), Mustafa and Garcia (2021), and Panigrahi et al. (2018). Each of these studies supports the use of the TAM model in MOOCs. The following sections contain additional research examples of TAM studied with MOOCs that align with and support this case study.

MOOCs Studied in Higher Education

MOOCs are heavily used by higher education resources that provide e-certifications as well as individual learners seeking knowledge and the transition into the workforce (Aljaraideh, 2019; Altalhi, 2021; Alyoussef, 2021; Baig, 2019; Liyanagunawardena et al., 2013; Salikhova et al., 2020; Zhu et al., 2020). MOOCs have gained a significant draw from higher education sectors due to their ability to address the gap between skills and academic knowledge gained in a higher education degree (Mendoza et al., 2017). In addition, e-learning approaches like MOOCs are ideal for meeting students' flexibility (Korepin et al., 2020). However, researchers indicate a need to understand how free courses, such as MOOCs, meet consumers' needs (Aljaraideh, 2019; Lim & Kim, 2018; Van Popta et al., 2017; Wang et al., 2019). Although certification is a popular business model in MOOCs, there are disadvantages to this model, such as associated fees no longer making it a free resource. Additionally, without a certification, individuals cannot gain proof of the necessary selection and skill training from MOOCs (Lewer et al., 2006).

Kalman (2014) studied MOOC applications to disrupt the business models of higher education sectors. For example, traditional universities offer multiple free looks compared to paid online courses offered by distance teaching universities (Kalman, 2014). Mendoza et al.

(2017) also argued that MOOC technology adoption improved understanding of how individuals and higher education resources can employ e-commerce-based resources to support online learning. However, Mendoza et al. (2017) also noted a need to improve these models to meet the needs of students, consumers, and adopting institutions. Improvements may include consumer perceived value and the adoption of changes in how knowledge is obtained (Baig, 2019).

MOOCs Studied in Technology Adoption and Acceptance

The adoption of MOOCs has enhanced student learning abilities but there are also concerns regarding students' ability to complete procedures based on their self-discipline (Ceron et al., 2020; Jovic et al., 2017; Sanni & Ajiboye, 2021). Altalhi (2021) analyzed MOOC and technology adoption, focusing on how these technologies have enhanced student learning and teachers' ability to guide educators through coursework. A total of 150 students were surveyed regarding the outcomes of MOOCs and the learning techniques used to enhance their application of learning strategies and student decision-making processes. The findings indicated that factors of self-efficacy and attitude are the most important for students' outcomes (Altalhi, 2021). In addition, the variables of social influence, effort, expectancy, and attitude were important facilitating variables supported by other researchers (Aggarwal et al., 2021; Altalhi, 2021; Baig, 2019; Seibert et al., 2021).

MOOCs Studied With Personality Traits

Understanding the relationship between personality and consumer satisfaction ensures success among students in MOOCs and can improve learning strategies (Baruth & Cohen, 2022; Matcha et al., 2020). Recent research contributes to the expanding knowledge of personality traits, continued use, and completion of MOOCs (Abdullatif & Velazquez-Iturbide, 2020; Gupta, 2021; Otero-Lopez et al., 2021; Zheng, 2020). Findings indicate a strong correlation between these factors and address the issue of dropout rates among students. Overall, there is a need to improve the understanding of consumer-based traits when studying the knowledge economy within the MOOC framework (Gupta, 2021; Mendoza et al., 2017; Salikhova et al., 2020).

Challenges and Critics of MOOC Learning

Challenges of MOOC application also include the inability of educators to adapt the course to student needs and the failure to engage students. Higher education programs depend greatly on the student's self-discipline and completion rate (Vorbach et al., 2019). In particular, the lack of instructor presence reduces learner commitment to the learning process. Self-directed students were more likely to succeed in the online classroom. Therefore, self-directed learning is essential in MOOCs for individuals to gain the necessary skills to succeed after graduation or bridge the gap between higher education and the workforce, and it could be a challenge for those lacking this ability.

Similarly, Thomas and Nedeva (2018) argued that the inclusion of MOOCs represented a symbiotic relationship in which the education technology sector relied on free resources to meet the universal learner audiences. For example, e-learning approaches are ideal for meeting students' flexibility requirements (Korepin et al., 2020; Li et al., 2017; Zhang et al., 2020). Thus, further research on consumer personality traits is required to understand how such programs can benefit consumers (Kim et al., 2021; Thomas & Nedeva, 2018).

Kim et al. (2021) reviewed the challenges noted among MOOCs by analyzing survey responses from 664 learners who took a large-scale MOOC class for the assessment. They found a relationship between core structure, organization, and self-directed learning commitment among students. In addition, the MOOC's usability may decrease students' ability to complete each course assignment and hinder their learning outcomes (Hanifa & Santoso, 2019; Kim et al.,

2021; Kung & Lee, 2017; Thomas & Nedeva, 2018). The findings indicated needed

recommendations to ensure students complete each course assignment and eliminate the

hindrance of learning outcomes (Hanifa & Santoso, 2019; Shi et al., 2018). Furthermore, critics

suggested that MOOCs would not address the challenges of reaching students from

disadvantaged backgrounds (Kalman, 2014).

There are challenges with MOOCs in the business industry as well. For example, Korepin

et al. (2020) gathered data through a sample of 1600 respondents across eighty regions of the

Russian Federation. They employed in-depth interviews with employees using MOOCs, top

managers, heads of units, mid-level managers, and employees. The findings indicated that there

is a need to further transform e-learning as a means to meet the new market requirements for

training specializations in digital logistics. Additionally, the findings indicated a continued need

for OPK-based programs that may improve employees' ability to meet the industries' skills and

management needs (Aljaraideh, 2019; Van Popta et al., 2017; Wang et al., 2019).

Critics of MOOCs in higher education also include Lewer et al. (2006), who researched

the use of MOOCs among universities across the globe. They noted a lack of sustainability due

to upfront creation costs and the inability to maintain costs and ensure that content is relevant.

The authors reported a need for further understanding consumer moderating variables to improve

long-term sustainability. These same concerns were mirrored by Liyanagunawardena et al.

(2013) and Liyanagunawardena et al. (2015). They also argued that although MOOCs offer

important services, they lack sustainability due to insufficient revenue and the costs associated

with running and rerunning the programs. These concerns indicate that while free MOOCs are

important, paid OPK may be more critical for the ability of consumers to reach their desired

goals (Lewar et al., 2006; Liyanagunawardena, 2015; Vorbach et al., 2019). Further, paid online modules and full degrees online are increasing due to the ability of students to complete, engage, and increase their satisfaction based on the offerings of these programs (Kim et al., 2021; Thomas & Nedeva, 2018).

MOOCs and Pricing Shifts Studied With TAM

MOOCs are an important example of free learning in the advanced Internet age (Almeda, 2018; El Mawas et al., 2018; Kung & Lee, 2017). Using the TAM theory with the MOOC experience helps identify antecedents of the model (Dai et al., 2021). The literature reviewed in this section clarifies behavior intention and consumer perceived value within the TAM theory.

Pricing behavior research focusing on MOOCs has indicated that this shift from free to paid learning is related to the changes in consumer consumption, satisfaction, and completion. (Littenberg-Tobias et al., 2020; Tareen & Haand, 2020; Wang et al., 2019). For example, Littenberg-Tobias et al. (2020) examined the relationship between pricing and learning behavior, focusing on online courses. The author employed two case studies to discuss how learner cohorts offered coupons for e-certificates as well as the influence of price reductions on the online learning setting of MOOC's. The first case study compared participation in certification rates and courses with and without free certification coupons and noted a higher sign-up rate for the free certification track. However, students have a higher completion rate in the paid certification process. In the second case study, the authors found that learning behavior intention was high among individuals that paid for certification. These findings indicate an important connection between paid and free knowledge, which may ultimately benefit the learner's outcome and completion rates in MOOCs (Littenberg-Tobias et al., 2020; Tareen & Haand, 2020; Wang et al., 2017).

However, individuals who do not pay for these programs also face reduced completion and satisfaction rates. (Hanifa & Santoso, 2019; Panigrahi et al., 2018). Shi et al. (2018) mirrored similar findings, noting that MOOCs have lacked a systematic price analysis, and the impact on consumers is significant. The authors emphasized a need to understand how price differences impact consumer completion and satisfaction rates and suggested further research on ensuring students complete each course (Almeda, 2018; El Mawas et al., 2018).

Paid online modules and full degrees are growing in popularity due to the ability of students to complete courses, engage with content, and increase satisfaction and the range of content in these programs (Thomas & Nedeva, 2018). Research indicates a need to understand further how products, such as OPKs, meet the needs of consumers (Korepin et al., 2020; Li et al., 2017). In addition, findings indicate a continued need for OPK-based programs that may improve the ability of employees to meet the demands of the industry and the management (Korepin et al., 2020; Li et al., 2017).

From Free to Paid

For a significant period, free online learning was a hallmark of online Internet offerings. However, as technology acceptance has become more widespread, consumer needs and wants to have changed, and online content has shifted from free to paid (Chen et al., 2021; Li et al., 2019; Peuler & McCallister, 2019; Punj, 2015; Raban et al., 2019; RuBell et al., 2020; Zykov, 2016). The continued use of content and e-learning programs through smartphones, tablets, and computers increased the ability of organizations to offer consumer-based courses that are either free or paid. The expansion of this technology provides relevance to the TAM theory.

Further, the digital content creation market is consistently growing globally (Ling, 2021). For example, data from SyndiGate Media Inc (2020) noted that there had been an increased growth of 16.8% from 2018 to 25% in terms of online learning. Chen et al. (2021) reported that the number of paid users on the Chinese platform, Zhihu, reached 360 million in China. In addition, a report from Global Market Insights indicated that the global online education market would reach $300 Billion by 2025 (Cornejo-Velazquez et al., 2019).

Gu et al. (2018) stated that the switch from free to paid programs aligned with increased sales and marketing strategy. In addition, consumers are more likely to pay for premium versions based on positive experiences with free platforms. Similarly, researchers noted that service providers that use free programming for sharing product information are also likely to see an increase in individuals willing to purchase paid material based on the effectiveness and satisfaction of free content. These findings indicate that using these programs can be effective for some organizations (Berger et al., 2015; Hoang et al., 2019). The following sections provide examples of TAM and technology acceptance in various settings using the "free to paid" concept.

From Free to Paid in Higher Education

Higher education facilities greatly benefited from free to low-cost courses as technology has developed. TAM is considered an effective theory for studying usage and behavior in higher education (Al-Qaysi et al., 2020). These programs can also disrupt the industries of low and mid-tier colleges that cannot use branding or regional advantages to gain access to these programs for the benefit of their students. For example, Scuderi (2018) performed a qualitative content analysis of three companies that offered free online or inexpensive courses using StraighterLine, Udacity, and Coursera platforms. Four key themes were identified from the content analysis: credentialing issues, the unbundling of higher education, the development of online learning, and single-course providers. Higher education programs noted similar benefits. For example, Clarke et al. (2018) indicated that programs, such as Google ad grants, which provide higher education facilities and publish ads, can improve students' skills development when adopting online learning technology.

However, there are multiple disadvantages to free courses that can ultimately disrupt the ability of certain higher education institutions to provide online learning for their students (Berger et al., 2015; Li et al., 2017; Huang, 2016; Scuderi, 2018). Mohammadi and Kinyo (2020) researched learning as a lifelong process and stated that formal education is no longer sufficient for business needs. With the availability of knowledge today and multiple learning opportunities beyond the traditional curriculum, there has been an increased need among adults to seek knowledge to increase their skills and economic advantages outside of the formal education process (Mohammadi & Kinyo, 2020). Platforms like Coursera, Udacity, StraighterLine provide disruptive innovations for higher education because they are cheaper, simpler, and more convenient (Scuderi, 2018).

From Free to Paid in Business Entities

As technology and technology acceptance progressed, the transformation from free to paid content included switching from free programs such as cloud computing, ad grants, and MOOCs to paid courses, platforms, and technological tools in businesses. This process initially started through consumers realizing the benefit of e-learning and tools and later desiring more advanced methods, demonstrating the TAM theory (Ahmed, 2020; Gu et al., 2018; Halbheer et al., 2014). For example, Ahmed (2020) studied cloud computing as a recent advancement in online-based web tools. The authors noted that cloud computing had gained traction over the past decade and has evolved into a paid online market. Further, cloud computing increased the ability of small and medium-sized enterprises to adapt to e-commerce-based processes.

Revenue streams continue to grow among content providers, such as news, media, and entertainment goods, as they expand into digital content (Gallaugher et al., 2001; Hoang et al., 2018). As a result, the experience goods industry has adapted its distribution channel, including music and movies. For example, due to digitization distribution, physical products such as CDs/DVDs have decreased sales (Khouja & Wang, 2010). Companies such as Spotify have capitalized on this opportunity and offer free service with the option to upgrade to paid service (Nusca et al., 2019). Other companies, such as Netflix, YouTube, and Hulu, follow similar patterns of free and paid options (Na et al., 2016).

Free Samples Leading to Paid Content

As online content has become the norm in technology adoption, a shift in strategy among producers allowed them to charge for content. As this was a natural progression, it was easier to earn the consumer's trust and build credibility by letting them experience the content before making a purchase. For example, Hinnawi and Mohammad (2018) provided a perspective on how online knowledge quickly transferred from free to paid platforms. The authors focus on the most used application and positive and negative roles in lifelong informal learning, including applications such as free sites and blogs. Regarding mediating factors, Hinnawi and Mohammad (2018) identified that knowledge, intellectual beliefs, education, and health and medicine were critical factors that impacted individuals' application and use of such sites.

Lambrecht et al. (2017) also demonstrated that free content is important to consumer behavior intention. There is a need to understand further how a transformation from free to paid content can ultimately impact the consumer and the organizing institution. For example, Gallaugher et al. (2001) found that online revenue streams are often characterized by the ability of organizations to impact consumer loyalty. Halbheer et al. (2014) also corroborated that selling digital information, such as magazines, was important to understanding free samples' benefits, ultimately increasing paid content purchases. However, a lack of information regarding consumer traits, such as paid and free content personality traits, limited this understanding (Ahmed, 2020; Halbheer et al., 2014).

From Free to Paid: Content Sampling and Technology Adoption

Consumers are also more likely to pay if they enjoy an initial product sample and find that it meets their needs. Therefore, online learning focusing on knowledge acceptance and consumer-based needs and how they process information with e-learning commerce is more likely to offer paid or low-cost services. (Park et al., 2020; Seitz et al., 2018). Consumers' willingness to pay and the ability to gain information succinctly and effectively were vital in transitioning from free to paid courses (Park et al., 2020). In addition, consumers are more likely to pay if they can access all services desired to learn information rather than search consecutively for services that provide their selected courses and information (Niemand et al., 2019; Park et al., 2020).

The switch from free to paid media aligned with market trends and indicated that offering sampled services was more likely to increase paid consumers (Li et al., 2019; Niemand et al., 2019; Park et al., 2020). For example, Meng et al. (2021) found that knowledge sharing in online health communities led to patient recruiting. The change from free to paid content was based on increased consumer desire to gain desired knowledge in a singular effective platform (Hoang et al., 2019; Kimura et al., 2018). This indicated that the consumption of digital information goods is aligned with using a content sampling strategy, in which individuals are provided a free portion of the content, most often leading to a likelihood to purchase paid content. This transition illustrates that while previously free services were adequate, the search among consumers has led to an increased application of paid services (Hoang et al., 2019; Kimura et al., 2018; Koch & Benlian, 2017).

The overall benefit of offering free services is the knowledge that consumers are more likely to purchase a paid product after becoming familiar with the service, specifically adopting the platform technology and being satisfied with the result (Hoang et al., 2019; Kimura et al., 2018; Koch & Benlian, 2017). This procedure applies to all marketing strategies but has overtaken the online learning market after shifting from free to paid content (Lambrecht et al., 2014). Zhang et al. (2019) argued that a firm's core product holds stand-alone value, but value-added services are only applicable if a free service is initially provided. Thus, an online service that offers a few free service levels is more likely to gain consumers to pay for their products after initial exposure to the e-learning platform (Zhang et al., 2019).

From Free to Paid: Price Sensitivity Demonstrating Perceived Value of the Theory

Zhang et al. (2019) further assessed factors influencing customer satisfaction regarding paid knowledge. The findings indicated that there is differential satisfaction based on their expertise. In particular, the results indicated that expert customers are less sensitive to price. Historically price positively influences the satisfaction of novice customers but negatively for expert customers (Zhang et al., 2019). Also, historically, satisfaction affects expert customers less, thus, indicating that paid services for online learning or more likely to be positively perceived by expert customers (Koch & Benlian, 2017; Zhang et al., 2019). This consideration implies that the process from free to paid knowledge adds value to the core product. However, there is a need to understand further how consumer consumption changes based on their personality and reliance on free or paid-based services (Hoang et al., 2019; Kimura et al., 2018; Koch & Benlian, 2017).

Digital Entrepreneurs Enter OPK Market Capitalizing on Technology Acceptance

A significant shift in the online learning market was the entrance of digital entrepreneurs (Agarwal, 2015; Hsieh et al., 2019; Kraus et al., 2019; Li et al., 2017; Sahut et al., 2021; Standing & Mattsson, 2018; Zaheer et al., 2019). Digital entrepreneurs are likely drawn toward the OPK-based frameworks, innovative desire processes, and focus on innovation and commercialization (Aldholay et al., 2018; Hsieh et al., 2019; Jahnke et al., 2020). The renewed understanding of the benefit of offering free content to gain the knowledge and interests of page consumers brought about interest from digital entrepreneurs to increase their ability to acquire consumers, profit, as well as benefit individuals seeking the OPK market (Elia et al., 2020; Li et al., 2017; Sahut et al., 2021).

Digital entrepreneurship developed during the digital revolution by individuals who were able to take actions that would benefit themselves based on new growth and market trends (Cornejo-Velazquez et al., 2019; Zhang et al., 2019). The process of digital learning is a process of micro-learning, which is attractive to entrepreneurs that attempt to meet the needs of consumers while cultivating a sustainable business model (Antonopoulou & Begkos, 2020; Jahnke et al., 2020; Ludeke-Freund, 2020). The development of this technology allowed digital entrepreneurs to focus on value propositions (Antonopoulou & Begkos, 2020).

Digital Entrepreneurs: Factors in e-Commerce

Srinivasan and Venkatraman (2018) emphasized that exploring entrepreneurship when researching digital platforms is important. In particular, the ability of individuals to coordinate across platforms aids in entrepreneurship success. Thus, digital entrepreneurship is intrinsically connected to a network-centric perspective. In addition, as consumers begin to share information on Q&A platforms, they also enter into a form of entrepreneurship (Park et al., 2020; Srinivasan & Venkatraman, 2018).

Previous findings indicate a gap in how individuals are likely to employ e-commerce-based programs that implement the technology without current knowledge (Beliaeva et al., 2019; Geissinger et al., 2019; Ghezzi & Cavallo, 2020). Alford et al. (2020) examined marketing technology from the perspective of small businesses. Surveys were distributed regarding their perceptions of arcane technology adoption. The findings indicated that the ability to adapt to these opportunities showed a reduction due to insufficient knowledge on implementing strategies while also gaining a return on investments.

Digital Entrepreneurs: Creating Value

Researchers argued that the introduction of digital entrepreneurship increased the need to understand the perceived value and the conceptualization of how the behavior of consumers interacts with the newly developed pay-based learning content and platforms (Guthrie, 2014). Rybakova and Nazarov (2021) argued that we need to understand how business and digital economic error can improve our understanding of market research and create differing policies for small and large companies globally. Similarly, Agarwal et al. (2015) examined the growth potential of e-commerce through an assessment of emerging economies. The authors found that institutional environment, infrastructure, and culture were essential for e-commerce growth development at a national level. In addition, the transactional level demonstrated the importance of multiple factors, such as the integrity of transactions, online intermediaries, network externalities, and value clustering.

Singh and Hussain (2021) further noted a need to provide improved information to support digital entrepreneurs, such as improving how individuals perceive value among e-learning platforms and tools. In addition, sellers of digital goods must consider different variables and terms of the desired consumable product, which initiated a growing increase in digital entrepreneurship over the past five years (Adomavicius et al., 2015; Freudenreich et al., 2020). Finally, Aldousari et al. (2016) examined consumer purchase attitudes regarding online shopping through three perspectives the technology acceptance model (TAM) and the theory of reasoned action (TRA). However, there is a gap in the research focusing on OPK in the framework of consumer attitudes with the TAM model. Additionally, research called for a qualitative study of personality traits in online courses, thus, further demonstrating the need for the current study (Aldholay et al., 2018; Hsieh et al., 2019; Jahnke et al., 2020; Usakli, 2019). As a result, there is a call for renewed research regarding personality traits, behavior, and the general perceptions of consumer value for e-learning products (Guthrie, 2014; Rybakova & Nazarov, 2021; Singh & Hussain, 2021).

From Free to Paid: Relevance to Current Study

In relevance to this current study, the shift from free to paid content demonstrates a renewed focus on OPK based on carriers' need to provide paid knowledge to meet consumer-based demand (Cornejo-Velazquez et al., 2019; Lambrecht et al., 2014; Lambrecht et al., 2017; Mohammadi & Kinyo, 2020; Sinha & Bagarukayo, 2019). Zhu and Zhang (2019) further analyzed knowledge payment by focusing on free knowledge on the number of purchases of paid knowledge from constant carrier platforms. In addition, Zhu and Zhang (2019) specifically focused on free and paid knowledge theory questions in Zhihu, a platform provided across China. The findings indicated that paid knowledge is more affected by the number of questions an individual asks (Zhu & Zhang, 2019).

Raban et al. (2019) examined the selection, evaluation, and integration of knowledge in online learning. The authors examined data from 106 university students. The students participated in an experiment regarding online information in which information was required to reach a disservice decision regarding a controversial topic. The findings indicated that individuals who provided paid information were more likely to have a more data-informed choice regarding the controversial topic. These findings indicate the importance of considering consumer-based traits, a key focus of this current study (Lissitsa & Kol, 2016; Na et al., 2016).

Su et al. (2019) also examined OPK by focusing on the transformation from providing free knowledge to online paid knowledge. In particular, the authors noted that there had been a sustainable and progressive movement toward the business model that focuses on consumers' online knowledge and purchase intention. Therefore, the authors focused on cognitive-affective and cognitive frameworks in conjunction with the customer value theory. Su et al. (2019) posed their idea within a survey of 504 respondents, which was analyzed using structural equation modeling. The findings indicated that consumer value and identification with knowledge contributors influenced their trust in the platform and purchase intentions of OPK products (Li et al., 2017; Su et al., 2019).

The preceding examples indicate that when considering the transition from free to paid knowledge, it is vital to consider consumer-based factors that impact trust and purchase intention (Li et al., 2017; Zahan et al., 2020). These findings further demonstrate the importance of consumer demand and mediating factors, such as personality traits and OPK characteristics (Raban et al., 2019; Hinnawi & Mohammad, 2018). However, there is a need to further expand these understandings of how mediating factors, such as personality traits and variables, impact the consumer's consumption of free or paid knowledge (Hoang et al., 2019; Kimura et al., 2018; Koch & Benlian, 2017; Zhu & Zhang, 2019).

Online Paid Knowledge (OPK) Market

The Online Page Knowledge (OPK) market is essential to address as the purpose of this study is an exploration of how different personality traits describe value within the construct of PU and PEOU of online courses in the online paid knowledge market using the contextual antecedents of OPK characteristics (Cai et al., 2020; Fang et al., 2021; Meng et al., 2021; Su et al., 2019). In addition, TAM has been used to explain certain aspects of the OPK market (Xu et al., 2021; Zhang et al., 2020). Therefore, the researcher reviewed relevant literature regarding OPK and discussed the importance of the study's purpose and previous knowledge using the TAM constructs of PU, PEOU, and consumer personality traits.

OPK: Current Trends

Contemporary research regarding current trends has indicated that the OPK market is relevant when examining consumer purchasing behaviors and trends (Cai et al., 2020; Hofacker, 2020; Rybakova & Nazarov, 2021; Zhang & Wu, 2019). Zhang and Wu (2019) researched the investment within the digital content industry in China from 2017 to 2018 and trends in content profit and digital services over five years. These trends include OPK, online education, online videos, live streaming, news, and online periodicals. In addition, the authors noted China's increasingly competitive layout regarding reaching OPK consumers and ensuring that consumers can purchase quality products that meet their needs.

Zhang and Wu (2019) also stated a current trend toward OPK within the digital content industry in China. The authors considered observations from the past ten years and noted that online content, especially paid content, is more prevalent among younger generations. Further, more individuals are seeking OPK in comparison to free knowledge services. However, these findings also demonstrated a gap in the reviewed literature regarding considering consumer behavior within the perspective of personality traits and OPK products, specifically in the United States (Cai et al., 2020; Chen et al., 2021; Zhang & Wu, 2019).

Sanchez and Hueros (2010) further emphasized that OPK-based platforms offer a unique insight into how the digitalization of services crossed both the public and private sectors. The authors specifically examine motivational factors regarding student satisfaction and dissatisfaction with the web-based learning program Moodle. The assessment included a survey of 226 students at the business administration and management in an infant and primary school teaching degree courses across the University of Huelva. The findings indicated that technical support was directly related to consumer's perceived ease of use and usefulness of the e-learning web-based application. Thus, it further supports the TAM model's reliability and application in exploring consumer behavior and user likeliness to adapt and use technology.

OPK: Studied With TAM

Previous literature demonstrates a lack of research on personality traits when considering PU and PEOU as moderators for OPK and online consumers (Fang et al., 2021; Meng et al., 2021; Su et al., 2019). Xu et al. (2021) examined OPK products within a TAM framework, focusing on pricing strategies for information products. Xu et al. (2018) considered complementary services for information products within a dualistic market. Further, several authors examined complementarily or network effects that enhance corporate profit based on intrinsic value (Meng et al., 2021; Xu et al., 2018). The authors noted that when considering OPK products, it is important to assess the organization's profitability and the network's inherent value (Su et al., 2019). In addition, trust and OPK identification within the knowledge economy is positively associated with purchaser intent (Fang et al., 2021; Meng et al., 2021; Su et al., 2019).

OPK: Sales and Driving Factors

Several studies have focused on the driving factors for OPK products by focusing on online sales and user-generated information in the knowledge-sharing community. (Cai et al. 2018; Pang et al., 2020; Zhang et al. 2019; Zhang & Zeng, 2014; Zhao et al., 2018; Zhao et al., 2020). Zhang and Zeng (2014) called for more research in defining knowledge expertise in the sharing economy, citing mass amateurization in the knowledge markets. The authors measured the ratings of contributor expertise, live broadcasts using signaling theory, as well as content products, follow-up content producers, and upvotes (positive reviews) on OPK content. According to Zhang et al. (2019), ratings and followers are positively impacted; however, upvotes negatively impact sales. The authors noted that this provides insight into product transactions and consumer behaviors. Conversely, Cai et al. (2018) found that likes improved sales in the sharing economy.

Zhao et al. (2018) examined payment decisions in terms of OPK through consideration of contributor characteristics and reputation effects. The authors collected data through a binomial panel regression model that considered data from websites in China. Zhao et al. (2018) also considered ability integrity by focusing on contributors' reputation and trustworthiness attributes. Findings indicated that user payment decision was positively affected by trustworthiness attributes. However, price positively moderates the relationship between user trust and payment decisions.

Purchasing intent among consumers regarding PU and PEOU when considering OPK products has some limited research (Xu et al., 2017; Yu et al., 2021; Zhang & Wu, 2019). Xu et al. (2017) examined OPK by focusing on Chinese students' intention to purchase using the TAM model. The authors surveyed 405 Chinese participants regarding their willingness to pay for online paid knowledge for the assessment. Those findings were examined using the structural equation model and frame through TAM. The research found that PEOU was positively associated with PU and attitudes. Further, PU and attitude were positively associated with purchasing intent (Xu et al., 2017).

Similarly, Cai et al. (2020) considered the sales of OPK through a two-phase model that examined data from an online Chinese website. First, the authors considered knowledge products through audio broadcasts and purchasing behavior after the initial broadcasting of the product. The findings indicated that price affects live sales and cumulative prior sales. Further, the review score and audience interactions affected sales (Cai et al., 2020). These findings indicate that when considering the marketability of items and OPK products, that is important to take into consideration consumer behavior as well as personality, which is discussed further in this study and throughout the themes presented in this literature review (Chen et al., 2021).

The purchase intention of OPK products is associated strongly with companies that acknowledge their fee pricing processes and are transparent with consumers (Jing & Lu, 2020; Su et al., 2019; Zhang et al., 2019). Jing and Lu (2020) similarly identified purchase intention by focusing on OPK products using the behavioral plan theory. For the assessment, the authors distributed 457 surveys regarding purchase intention, characteristics of OPK products, and insertion recognition of copyright and fee payments. The findings indicate that variables of perceptive ease of use and planned behavior positively impacted purchase intention. Also, Kuang et al. (2019) studied non-incentivized user engagement by focusing on the OPK exchange platform using an archival data set from a major online knowledge exchange platform. Finally, a quasi-natural experiment examined OPK, financial incentives, and engagement (Kuang et al., 2019). The results indicated that paid knowledge-sharing activities motivated users to share more knowledge, increasing platform engagement voluntarily, thus, indicating positive effects regarding financial incentives for individuals to share within such platforms (Dhanesh & Duthler, 2019; Fang et al., 2021).

OPK: Consumer Perceived Value

Value creation in the content industry is a key factor for growth in the digital content industry (Agarwal, 2015; Berger et al., 2015; Huang, 2016; Li et al., 2017; Punj, 2015). Research, such as Su et al. (2019), examined OPK products by focusing on survey data from 504 respondents using consumer value theory. In particular, the study aimed to consider how trust develops during the affective stage, which leads to purchase decisions. The results indicated that customer value and identification with the knowledge contributor significantly influence trust and OPK products. Similarly, Molinillo et al. (2021) and Jin and Xu (2020) indicated a need to further understand the added value of products for the market and improve consumer-based research. For example, Molinillo (2021) investigated OPK by analyzing the procedures and evaluation of e-learning rewards. For their assessment, the authors specifically focused on gathering, defining, categorizing, classifying, and evaluating digital educational products underneath the category of OPK. The authors drew from the system success model using survey methods from 450 individuals for the assessment. The findings were analyzed using structural equation modeling. Jin and Xu (2020) indicated that system, information, and service quality are statistically associated with perceived utilitarian value. However, service quality and new product novelty do impact hedonic value among paid knowledge platforms.

There is a gap in literature that illustrates other consumer-based behaviors and personalities regarding payment decisions and trust within a particular brand or OPK-based technology (Cai et al., 2020; Chen et al., 2021; Zhang & Wu, 2019). These findings indicate a need to understand further user satisfaction and loyalty in OPK (Jin & Xu, 2020; Molinillo, 2021). Additionally, these findings demonstrate the current knowledge regarding OPK products and the need to consider further personality-based factors (Jin & Xu, 2020). Therefore, this study discussed the perceived value and personality traits in the OPK market.

Application of TAM and FFM to the Current Study

The literature review shows a gap in understanding personality traits and the consumers' perceived value in the OPK market (Bahl et al., 2019; Bandera et al., 2020; Mohammadi, 2015; Seibert et al., 2021). Research indicates that personality traits are important considerations with TAM to explain the impact of variables, which were largely unexplored in past research (Alonso & Romero, 2017; Su et al., 2019; Usakli, 2019). The FFM model has also been measured in relevance to PU and PEOU (Barnett, 2015). Therefore, the study used the TAM and the FFM framework as a guide to consider PU and PEOU in the OPK market (Harb & Alhayajneh, 2019; McElroy, 2007; Su et al., 2019; Svendsen et al., 2013).

The literature review includes understanding how personality traits affect user acceptance of technology (Barnett et al., 2015; Bento et al., 2019; Chen, 2011; Daljeet et al., 2017; Devaraj et al., 2008; Harb & Alhayajneh, 2019; Lui et al., 2020). In addition, personality traits described within the FFM are used in the qualitative study and contribute to the current body of research (Daljeet et al., 2017; Lui et al., 2020; Usakli, 2019). Together, the individual's personality traits, PU and PEOU, coalesce into the product's perceived value (Alonso & Romero, 2017; Marbach et al., 2019).

Research regarding TAM and FFM in online learning focused on the transformation of online learning and the creation of the OPK market in the past two decades. In addition, previous researchers elucidated the importance of understanding consumer behavior toward online products and OPK (Li et al., 2017; Li et al., 2019). Finally, previous research on current trends in the OPK market reviewed includes differing digital content resources, changes in market brands, as well as consumer perceptions of various OPK platforms and resources (Huo & Li, 2022; Xu et al., 2017; Xu et al., 2018; Zhang et al., 2019; Zhang & Wu, 2019; Zhou et al., 2022; Zhu, X., & Zhang, W., 2019).

The TAM and FFM theoretical models are important for improving market research understandings regarding consumer use, perceived ease of use, and the personality factors of individuals that use online shopping tools. However, there is a need to extend this to include the OPK market further and meet the previous recommendations regarding understanding PU, PEOU, and perceived value regarding personality characteristics within the framework of OPK products (Barr, 2018; Owens et al., 2019; Riccelli et al., 2017).

The study extended the literature of the OPK market to provide a renewed understanding of the FFM and TAM frameworks in exploring the contextual antecedents of course characteristics. In addition, the findings of this study may be beneficial for market-based knowledge and behavior research to improve the understanding of how PU and PEOU are mediators for OPK products of consumers in the United States. As noted by Bahl et al. (2019), Fu et al. (2020), Jin et al. (2020), Jing et al. (2020), Seibert et al. (2021), and Su et al. (2019), further research is needed to examine the understanding of personality traits and the consumer's perception of value using the TAM framework. At the same time, Usakli (2019) called for a qualitative study to further examine personality traits in online shopping, particularly beyond higher education. Finally, Zhou et al. (2022) call for future studies in the OPK market using consumer characteristics and environmental factors. Based on this literature review, the merits of the research problem are justified by synthesizing previous research and identifying gaps in previous studies.

Summary

Online shopping has grown significantly in the past two decades with advancements in technology and the Internet (Changchit et al., 2019). Research demonstrates that the widespread availability of the Internet has improved understanding of how consumers prefer to use technology and their behaviors (Fernandes et al., 2021). This literature review began with a technology acceptance model (TAM) overview and background, seminal research, critics, and the theoretical framework. The TAM model provides a framework for understanding the adoption and usage of technology based on the consumer. Additionally, supporting foundational theories related to TAM and other behavior theories not used in the current study are reviewed.

The next section of this literature review focused on the five-factor model (FFM) of personality traits. As noted, the FFM has been used to understand consumer behavior and the impact on usability and perceived ease of use (Devaraj et al., 2008). A review of the FFM framework provides reliability and structure for assessing consumers' personality traits. Research indicates that personality factors are important variables when considering technology adoption and online shopping (Zhou et al., 2007). Next, research and examples of literature using the TAM and FFM models together clarify the construct of research using both models in the current study. However, there remains a gap in literature regarding the TAM and FFM model intersection within the OPK market (Fu et al., 2020; Seibert et al., 2021; Su et al., 2019).

An overview of online learning and its history provide relevant background and context for the current study. In addition, MOOCs are a precursor for OPK in the knowledge economy (Baig, 2019). MOOCs are generally flexible and accessible for the user to use. However, MOOCs have experienced critiques from previous researchers regarding limitations for engagement and consumer completion rates (Choudhury, 2020; Littenberg-Tobias et al., 2020). These findings indicate that while MOOCs can positively contribute to online learning and gaining knowledge, a renewed understanding of consumer behavior and personality impact on PU and PEOU is needed.

The following section focused on the transition from free to paid knowledge through Internet evolution and technological progression, as well as the transition from free to paid among digital entrepreneurs. There have been multiple programs that started as open networks and changed to paid programs (Zhang et al., 2019). The available data indicates that consumers are most likely to pay for a service after they have sampled and experience the free service that meets their desires, needs, and wants. Research within this section demonstrated that online learning, traditionally free, moved towards paid programs due to the need to meet consumers' desires (Raban et al., 2019).

Researchers also illustrate a need to understand how such programs impact business models and can be improved to meet the needs of small and large organizations (Gregori & Holzmann, 2020; Rybakova, 2021). As the shift occurred from free to paid content, there was also an increase in digital entrepreneurs who could take advantage of the shifting business model (Li et al., 2017). As a result, entrepreneurship has renewed digital revolutions and has increased our understanding of consumer behavior market research online. Also, the entrance of digital entrepreneurs has led to further empirical questions regarding how organizations can meet the needs of consumers while also predicting their usability and adaption of specific technologies (Abyaa et al., 2019).

The last section of the literature review focused on applying TAM and the FFM in the OPK market. Specifically, the researcher considered how PU, PEOU, and personality traits of the consumer moderate OPK products among consumers in the United States. This phenomenon aimed to understand further how personality traits can describe PU and PEOU among consumers of OPK as a contribution to the existing literature in marketing research and expand the theoretical construct of the TAM and FFM.

In the reviewed literature, there is a lack of understanding regarding personality traits and how consumers perceive usefulness and perceived ease of use for OPK products among consumers in the United States (Bahl et al., 2019; Fu et al., 2020; Jin et al., 2020; Jing et al., 2020; Qi et al., 2019; Seibert et al., 2021; Su et al., 2019; Xu et al., 2021). Existing literature focuses on the impacts of the knowledge platform (Ivanova, S., 2018; Kuang et al., 2019; Li et al., 2017; Ling, J., 2021), products (Khaled et al., 2021; Zhao et al., 2018), content creation (Cai et al., 2020; Li et al., 2019), digital entrepreneurship (Abyaa et al., 2019; Seitz et al., 2018), as well as payments and purchase intention (Jing et al., 2020; Qi et al., 2019; Shi et al., 2020; Su et al., 2019; Zhang et al., 2020; Zhou et al., 2020; Zhu et al., 2019). However, the reviewed literature demonstrates a need for a deeper understanding of how personality traits perceive value within the TAM constructs of PU and PEOU for online courses in the OPK market.

Previous research has employed the FFM and TAM in quantitative studies (Barnett et al., 2015; Harb & Alhayajneh, 2019). However, a more detailed approach is needed using a qualitative method (Usakli, 2019). In the following section, the researcher introduces chapter 3, an overview of the design and methodology that guides the study. Chapter 3 includes multiple areas discussing instrumentation, study design, and methodology. The researcher also discusses

the data collection and analysis methods in Chapter 3.

Chapter 3: Research Method

The problem in this study addressed the question of how personality traits of consumers

perceive value of OPK products using perceived usefulness (PU) and perceived ease of use

(PEOU) as constructs among consumers in the United States (Bahl et al., 2019; Fu et al., 2020;

Jin et al., 2020; Jing et al., 2020; Seibert et al., 2021; Su et al., 2019). Su et al. (2019) cited the

need for further inquiry to understand how perceived value in the OPK market is affected by

personality traits. Similarly, Bahl et al. (2019) and Seibert et al. (2021) expressed a need for

further research on more specific technologies related to personality traits rather than technology

in general. Several studies have called for further research on the TAM model, including

investigating user perspectives in e-learning (Mohammadi, 2015) and further exploration of

product characteristics: service quality, information quality, and system quality (Jin, 2020). In a

study on knowledge products in China, Fu et al. (2020) suggested future research on knowledge

products and consumer satisfaction from other countries. Failure to understand personality traits

within the constructs of OPK characteristics as well as their perception of value could result in

failed marketing strategies among digital entrepreneurs as competition in the OPK market

continues to grow (Beig et al., 2019; Fu et al., 2020; Kraus, 2018; Marbach et al., 2016;

Matarazzo, 2021; Su et al., 2019).

Many studies have focused on online shopping behavior, including willingness to

purchase (Berger et al., 2015; Bucko et al., 2018; Li et al., 2017; Rajani, 2019). Purchase

intention factors, such as perceived risk (Biucky et al., 2017), perceived value (Gvili et al.,

2020), and perceived use (Ha et al., 2019), are a few topics researched in the online market.

Agarwal (2015) and Huang (2016) researched e-commerce within the technology adoption

framework. Watjatakul (2020) determined that different personality traits affect the perceived value and intention to adopt online courses. However, there is limited research in the literature exploring personality traits and technology interaction with digital learning products sold by for-profit businesses (Bento et al., 2019; Bruso et al., 2020; Regele, 2020; Zhou, 2022). This study sought to address this problem by discussing how personality factors (agreeableness, openness, conscientiousness, neuroticism and extroversion) impact consumer's perceived value, PU, and PEOU within the contextual antecedents of OPK product characteristics (Goldberg, 1990; Jin, 2020; Watjatrakul, 2020).

This chapter includes the research methodology, design and methods for the study. A qualitative descriptive case study design guided the study, and the chapter begins with a review of qualitative research. Other research methodologies, such as, mixed methods, quantitative, and variations of qualitative research, were reviewed and provided justification for the study. Next is a justification for the case study design. This chapter also describes the population, sample size, and materials used. Further, the method includes a description of study procedures and data analysis for this study provides detail for participant recruitment, participant notification, and informed consent. As with any research design, there were assumptions, limitations and delimitations. This section of the chapter includes an explanation of these as well as ethical assurances to ensure validity and credibility.

Research Methodology and Design

Research methodology clarifies the procedure of a study. Using a qualitative methodology could turn a given phenomenon into a set of representations using inductive exploration and other materials that help individuals comprehend a given situation and expand the body of existing research (Bloor & Wood, 2006; Dulock, 1993; Fox & Bayat, 2008; Sibeoni et al., 2020; Yin, 2016). Qualitative researchers focus on participants and how individuals make sense of their environment and experiences to describe a phenomenon (Lambert & Lambert, 2012; Meriam, 2020). According to Sandelowski (2000), qualitative studies emphasize *what*, *how*, and *why* phenomena occur in ways quantitative research cannot by using descriptive analysis.

Qualitative Methodology

The purpose of qualitative research is to discover distinctions of a phenomenon, and it is characterized by its focus or intention (Aspers et al., 2019; Maxwell, 2012; McCusker & Gunaydin, 2015). This method focuses on a small number of people, their experiences, and their behaviors. It addresses questions that provide insight into a particular phenomenon (Braun & Clark, 2022, Maxwell, 2012). One of the strengths of qualitative research is its primary goal to gain a detailed understanding rather than a generalization of people or settings (Maxwell, 2012; Sale, 2022). Consequently, qualitative research is an open-ended approach with design flexibility and creates the ability to gain meaningful insights (Braun & Clarke, 2022).

Qualitative research contributes to the existing body of knowledge by expanding conceptions and understandings of a phenomenon. Qualitative research design can be complex in several ways. First, the need to demonstrate validity and credibility is paramount (Yin, 2016). Creswell and Miller (2000) stated that the researcher's choice for validity considers audiences, their availability, and their use expense. Data triangulation ensures credibility in qualitative research (Korstjens et al., 2018). In addition, data triangulation aims to support data saturation (Mason, 2010).

Additionally, critics of qualitative research commonly cite transferability as a problem (Bloomberg, 2018; Korstjens et al., 2018). The fundamental concept of qualitative research is for the researcher to recognize patterns among data collected from interviews or other collection tool and then decide what is relevant to the study. As the interpretation of the data can be subjective, it can be difficult to replicate (Leung, 2015).

Similarly, Castleberry and Nolen (2018) stated that a challenge in qualitative research is the open-ended nature of data collection and the difficulty of reducing that to patterns. The limits of replication in qualitative research differ from quantitative research because the qualitative design does not seek transferability (Stahl et al., 2020). However, patterns and descriptions from one study can be applied to other studies using a systematic qualitative inquiry such as Braun and Clark's inductive thematic analysis (Braun & Clark, 2006). This consistency in the research leads to credibility in the findings (Shufutinsky, 2020).

Another difficulty in qualitative analysis is that there are multiple ways to approach a study, and there is no universal best way to approach a study (Belotto, 2018; Braun & Clarke, 2006; Sibeoni et al., 2020). In addition, the nature of qualitative analysis involves compiling data, interpreting, and drawing conclusions. Using qualities of research ensures reasonable interpretation (Yin, 2016). Qualities include complete interpretation, fair, accurate, and representative of raw data in context with current literature, and methods should be credible (Castleberry & Nolen, 2018).

Some common design approaches in qualitative research include grounded theory, ethnography, narrative research, phenomenology, and case study (Bohnsack et al., 2010; Bowen, 2009; Charmaz & Bryant, 2010; Sibeoni et al., 2020). Grounded theory (Glaser & Strauss, 1973; Nasrabadi et al., 2020) is a method to gather and analyze data simultaneously, conceptualize information, and develop new or extended theories (Glaser, 2022). Ethnography and narrative research focus on real-life implications (Bamber, 2021). Ethnography attempts to understand groups or cultures and their activities, and narrative research uses the participants' voices to tell a story (Cassell et al., 2018; Herring et al., 2016, Maxwell, 2012). The narrative design's purpose is to describe individual stories (Connelly & Clandinin, 2006).

Phenomenological design approaches examine a particular experience and the interactions with people (Cassell et al., 2018; Churchill & Wertz, 2015; Yin, 2016). According to Moustakas (1994), a phenomenological research design focuses on describing participants' practical lived experiences of an event toward a given phenomenon. Hofacker and Goldsmith (2020) used a phenomenological approach to marketing theory, citing that in addition to goods and services, there should be a third component of "information." Further, a phenomenological research design was used to investigate the personality traits of nurse managers (Alan & Baykal, 2021). The researchers found that the nurse managers' conscientiousness personality traits had the highest scores.

Case study design examines a particular phenomenon and is suitable when there are several types of data (Yin, 2013). An instrumental case study protocol allows for the exploration of a particular situation while providing a deeper insight into a situation or phenomenon (Yin, 2016). While all are valuable approaches in qualitative research, a case study design method aligns with the research questions to understand the phenomenon of the OPK market (Aagaard, 2017; Reeves et al., 2008, Williams, 2021, Yin, 2013).

Other Methodology: Mixed Methods

The mixed-method methodology was also considered for the study. Mixed methods combines qualitative and quantitative research in a single study (Maxwell, 2012). Researchers use a mixed-method approach when there is a need to provide an exhaustive understanding of a phenomenon using various configurations by integrating qualitative and quantitative methods. (Creswell, 2010; Sandelowski, 2000; Tashakkori & Creswell, 2007). An approach to mixed methods often used in social sciences research is the Fuzzy Set Qualitative Analysis approach (fsQCA). For example, Bawack et al. (2021) used fsQCA to study personality traits and the customer experience in online shopping, while Zhu et al. (2020) used fsQCA to study personality traits of entrepreneurs and new venture performance. Similarly, Pflugner et al. (2020) used the fsQCA strategy to study personality traits and technostress. The purpose of the study was to determine various configurations, and the mixed methods were the appropriate method given the variables. Further, the mixed methods were chosen over the qualitative research method because multiple variants, such as personality profiles and different exposures causing stress, were analyzed.

Critics of mixed methods cite the structure to include a hierarchy of quantitative over qualitative, placing higher importance on the quantitative aspects of the research (Creswell, 2010; Fabregues et al., 2021). In addition, Tashakkori and Teddlie (2003) addressed theoretical perspectives, citing that mixed methods are not interpretive enough to demonstrate transferability. Thus, given the focus of this study, the mixed-method approach is deemed inappropriate because the purpose of this study is not to gather numeric data but rather a rich description to understand the phenomenon further by gathering details of the participant's experience.

Other Methodology: Quantitative

A quantitative research method is used by researchers when the study focuses on collecting and analyzing numerical and statistical data. It attempts to explain a situation through variables and their statistical relationships (Maxwell, 2012). Additionally, Merriam (2016) argued that quantitative research methodology involves a researcher investigating the relationship between variables by testing hypotheses and theories. For example, Alduaij (2019) analyzed 250 online surveys on TAM and trends in social media adoption to generalize social media in the Kuwait population. Finally, quantitative methods use large amounts of volume to represent a structured analysis of the population (Chrysochou, 2017).

There are some similarities in practice between qualitative and quantitative research, such as data gathering designs (Aspers et al., 2019; Chrysochou, 2017; Flick et al., 2004). For example, both methods often use in-depth surveys and focus groups. Conversely, qualitative and quantitative research methods have two different approaches to research and serve different purposes (Chrysochou et al., 2017; Flick et al., 2004). For example, in quantitative analysis, large amounts of data are typically collected to generalize data as part of the research objective (Chrysochou, 2017). In comparison, qualitative research does not aim to generalize the population but looks at a phenomenon more in its natural environment using small population samples (Williams, 2021).

Qualitative methodology does not reduce the data to numbers and variables, limiting the ability to gather new observations. Instead, it focuses on the human experience and presents its findings as themes rather than a cause-effect relationship (Aspers et al., 2019; Franzosi, 2010; Maxwell, 2012; Willig, 2019). Therefore, the quantitative research method did not align with this study's research questions and purpose. Therefore, quantitative research methodology is incompatible with the current study because the aim of the research questions called for an exploratory approach to the OPK market phenomenon.

Qualitative Methodology For this Study

This study focused on the impact of consumer's personality traits and their perceived value of OPK and its characteristics. Approaching the research questions qualitatively provides more clarity and a more meaningful understanding of different personality traits and perceptions of online courses (Bamberg, 2021; Huyler et al., 2019; Utami et al., 2020; Usakli, 2019; Yin, 2016). For example, investigation techniques used in this study included surveys, semi-structured interviews, and exploratory data analysis. This study used a qualitative descriptive case study, as called for by Usakli (2019), to extend the TAM theory by exploring consumer perceived value using personality traits as antecedents within the boundaries of the OPK market.

Previous research supported the combined use of TAM and the FFM model (Barnett et al., 2015; Devaraj et al., 2008; Harb et al., 2019; Prasetya et al., 2015; Svendsen et al., 2013). Similar to these studies, the TAM Model serves as the theoretical framework. Additionally, the FFM establishes the personality traits of participants as antecedents to be studied. This study extended the literature by using this construct to examine the OPK market further. (Bahl, 2018; Barr, 2018; Fu et al, 2020; Jin et al., 2020; Jing et al., 2020; Owens et al., 2019; Riccelli et al., 2017; Seibert et al, 2021; Su et al., 2019). Therefore, the research questions align with the descriptive case study design by aiming to gain rich data regarding how personality traits perceive value and course characteristics in the OPK market (Goldberg, 1990; Jin, 2020; Watjatrakul, 2020).

The qualitative methodology was best suited for this study because it can capture the complexity of the phenomena and describe how different personality traits perceive various OPK characteristics as perceived value. In addition, a descriptive case study research design is suitable for exploring the current topic and research questions. Therefore, the qualitative case study research design was the most appropriate for this study because the researcher intended to provide an opportunity for consumers who purchase online courses to assess their personality type and describe the OPK course characteristics they perceive to be useful and easy to use (Huyler et al., 2019; Yin, 2016).

Design Methods and Approach for This Qualitative Study

A qualitative descriptive case study is a design focused on current issues or problems through a data collection process that enables them to describe the situation in depth (Bamberg, 2021; Bloomberg, 2018; Bloor, 2006; Yin, 2013). Lambert and Lambert (2012) defined a descriptive case study research design as a method of inquiry that seeks to describe a given population, circumstances, or phenomenon investigated (Williams, 2021). The case study approach discusses accounts of an experience (Castleberry & Nolen, 2018; Churchill & Wertz, 2015). The design for this study identified antecedents (personality traits) and added to the literature by creating a holistic, overarching view of the OPK market phenomena within the TAM framework (Ajibade, 2018; Goldberg, 1990; Jin, 2020; Watjatrakul, 2020). The study's purpose was a deeper exploration of perceived value in the OPK market using personality traits as antecedents. Using the TAM model, interview questions discussed how personality traits and OPK course characteristics perceive value.

The researcher collected data through semi-structured interviews exploring participant's descriptions and explanations of the course characteristics and how their personality traits, PU, and PEOU perceived value. The design was compatible with research questions that seek to explain how the five personality trait factors impact consumer perception of online course characteristics and how the five personality trait factors and the online course characteristics affect consumer perceived value using the constructs of PU and PEOU. The data collected did not involve calculating numerical values, as in a quantitative study. Instead, the investigator examined various patterns and trends relating to the descriptions provided by the selected participants through semi-structured interviews. Therefore, quantitative research methodology was incompatible with the current study because the aim of the research questions calls for an exploratory approach to the OPK market phenomenon.

Using a case study design, this study's data and collection analysis used an inductive thematic analysis approach (Bloor & Wood, 2006; Braun & Clark, 2006; Williams, 2021). Sibeoni et al. (2020) describe it as "the study of what appears." This methodology is appropriate for this study because it allowed the researcher to understand the phenomenon within the chosen theoretical framework (Belotto, 2018). In addition, the researcher discussed how consumers' personality traits impact their interaction with online courses and the characteristics the courses exhibit (Churchill & Wertz, 2015).

Boundaries of Case Study

Boundaries help clarify the phenomenon for the study. In an exploratory case study, boundaries establish the main aspects of the case and lay the groundwork for research (Bloomberg, 2018). Boundaries for this case study allowed for a focused exploration of consumer perceived value in the OPK market. As such, boundaries for this study included United States residents aged 18 or older who have purchased online knowledge products such as webinars or courses from 2018–2021, courses were not from colleges and universities, and consumers who had access to the Internet.

Population and Sample

Since its inception in 2016, the knowledge payment industry has grown exponentially and has attracted attention from academics and practitioners (Fu et al., 2020; Qi et al., 2019; Zhang et al., 2019; Zhang et al., 2020; Zhao, 2020; Zhou et al., 2022). The global education market was estimated to be over $300 billion in 2019 (Cornejo-Velazquez et al., 2020). However, knowledge products continue to be part of an emerging business model and data regarding actual market size is somewhat limited (Chan et al., 2021; Fu et al., 2020). There are

countless providers of online courses and platforms outside of higher education. However, two

prominent platform providers for online courses outside of formal education are Coursera and

Udemy. Coursera listed the United States as their top market, with 16 million learners, valued at

$7 Billion in 2020. Udemy is another for-profit platform with approximately 30 million learners

(Cornejo-Velazquez et al., 2020). Another popular platform for digital entrepreneurs is Kajabi.

Kajabi, a U.S. based company, is a popular platform for entrepreneurial course creators. In their

2022 State of the Creator Economy Report, they reported over $3.5 Billion in earned income for

entrepreneurs using their platform (Kajabi, 2022).

The sample for the study comprised of consumers who have purchased OPK courses in

businesses in the online marketplace in the United States from 2018–2021. Using Facebook as

the primary source for recruitment, the researcher used a purposeful sample to examine the

phenomena. According to the annual data report by Kepios, Ltd., the estimated number of

Facebook accounts in the United States in 2021 was 7.1 million (Kepios, 2022). Of these,

approximately 3.7 million use online video as a source of learning, and approximately 1.9

million 27.7% (526,000) of these use social media to find inspiration for things to do and buy.

The research included a sample of 22 participants. Charmaz (2012) recommended 20 or

more participants for qualitative studies as enough for data analysis and saturation. Galvin (2021)

offered criteria for an appropriate number of interviews in qualitative research, citing 11–15

being the most common number of interviews required, and stated that data saturation is

achieved when the study can be replicated. Guest et al. (2020) supported this finding and found

that inductive studies, such as this study, are determined by the researcher.

Further, Galvin (2021) found that it is difficult to achieve true random sampling, so obtaining a representation of the types of people studied is beneficial. Therefore, this study used purposeful sampling to represent the big five personality traits (Yin, 2016). Using the survey questionnaire for demographic and personality information aided in the purposeful sampling and ensured that each of the big five personality traits were represented in the study and ensured that the sample size was sufficient for data saturation (Barnett et al., 2015; Creswell and Miller, 2000). The ability to replicate the study with this purposeful sample size assured data saturation (Fusch & Ness, 2015; Hennink & Kaiser, 2022). Additionally, this sample size assured the validity and transferability of this study (Bloomberg, 2018; Geist & Hitchcock, 2014).

In summary, the purposeful sample size allowed the researcher to gather rich and meaningful data to understand how different personality traits describe value by exploring OPK course characteristics using the TAM model of PU and PEOU. Participants were recruited primarily through Facebook, emails, social messaging, word of mouth, and electronic flyers on social media. Subjected to the inclusion and exclusion criteria outlined in Appendix B, a purposive sample of 22 participants were recruited. Furthermore, a detailed description of the sampling technique promoted data transferability.

Materials

Participants received an informed consent form (see Appendix B) detailing the study's purpose, objectives, parties' roles, and how the results were used. The consent form also provided a framework for participants' privacy and confidentiality, including using pseudonyms to avoid disclosing participants' identities to third parties. After selecting participants, a short survey captured demographic and foundational information. The survey was conducted before the interview. Initial, primary qualifying included, "Have you purchased an OPK course from 2018–2021?" and other questions from Appendix B, as well as basic demographic questions.

Additionally, the survey included questions for the personality assessment and was taken directly from the five-factor model (FFM) of personality traits. These were qualifying questions to establish purposive sampling, and data was included as antecedents in the exploration of the study. Caprara et al. (1993) introduced the "big five questionnaire" as a measurement tool to assess personality traits. The International Personality Item Pool Big Five (IPIP-B5) is a public domain developed based on Goldberg's personality inventory (1992) and was used to establish dominant personality traits (Appendix C). It contains personality assessment questions and scoring guidelines to assess the dominant personality traits of the participants (IPIP-B5).

The big five questionnaire is a proven reliable analysis to assess personality traits and was used in the initial survey (Abe, 2020; Abyaa et al., 2019, Gvili et al., 2019; McCrae et al., 2007; PsychTests AIM, I., 2011; Usakli, 2019). For example, Barnett (2015) used this instrument to understand the link between personality traits and the unified theory of acceptance and use of technology (UTAUT). Devaraj et al. (2008) also used this tool to research Information Systems and personality traits. Therefore, no pilot study was needed because this is an established method for assessing personality traits.

Researchers use a qualitative descriptive research approach, such as interviews, to gather detailed information about the phenomenon studied (Cassell et al., 2018; Merriam et al., 2016). Interviews allow data to be collected based on users' experiences (Barnham, 2015; Galletta, 2013; Marshall, 2013). The research method used semi-structured interviews to collect data in this inductive thematic study. Using open-ended questions allowed for data to be collected that established similarities between participants, allowing the researcher to recognize patterns and themes (Barnham, 2015). Other studies have successfully used similar instruments in studies of this nature, such as Endres et al. (2020), Gegenfurtner (2020), and Li (2017). Lisichkova et al. (2017) also successfully used personal interviews in conducting research using the TAM Model. Therefore, semi-structured interviews were the most valuable data source for the study.

The semi-structured interviews addressed the research questions, including "How do the five personality trait factors (agreeableness, openness, neuroticism, conscientiousness, extroversion) impact consumer perception of online course characteristics (system quality, information quality, service quality)?" and "How do the five personality trait factors (agreeableness, openness, neuroticism, conscientiousness, extroversion), and the online course characteristics (system quality, quality, service quality) affect consumer perceived value using the constructs of perceived usefulness (PU) and perceived ease of use (PEOU)?" In this study, semi-structured interviews were adequate because the researcher aimed to provide detailed descriptions of how different personality traits perceive value of OPK courses within the constructs of the TAM model. To ensure that the interviews addressed the required issues, experts from the dissertation committee reviewed interview questions as part of the proposal to ensure that wording was connected to the study's problem statement and managed the intended purpose.

To increase the study's validity, the researcher recorded interviews and took field notes during the interviewing process. A member study's validity was used to assess participants' responses to the narration accuracy to ensure that the final analysis represented their accurate descriptions. Participants had three days from the interview day to facilitate the member-checking process through email. No participants had any corrections to request. The research instruments and credibility were reviewed in the study procedures section below.

Study Procedures

Study procedures began with permission to conduct the study from the NCU's IRB. This included the IRB application and relevant materials such as the proposal summary, objectives, and purpose. Next, an expert panel consisting of the Academic Committee reviewed the interview questions, and the IRB reviewed the data collection instruments. The purpose was to ensure that the interview questions were well-worded and addressed the research questions. After the research proposal was approved, the researcher posted an invitation to participate in the study on Facebook and Instagram. In addition, flyers, emails, and word of mouth invited participants to the study as deemed appropriate.

Potential participants were required to contact the researcher. After expressing interest in participating in the study, the participant's eligibility was determined (see Appendix B). Successful participants were informed, and the researcher asked participants to sign the consent form electronically. Next, participants were asked to participate in a short (10-minute) online survey consisting of demographic and qualifying information.

The survey also contained a self-report questionnaire based on the big five questionnaire to establish a baseline of participants' personality traits (Goldberg, 1990). The big five questionnaire is a widely used instrument to measure personality traits: extraversion, agreeableness, conscientiousness, neuroticism, and openness to experience (Bagby & Widiger, 2018; Barnett et al., 2015; Boyle, 2008; Caprara et al., 1993; Chehreh et al., 2017; Chung et al., 2018; Devaraj et al., 2008; Gvili et al., 2019; McCrae & Costa, 2008; McCrae, 2009; Smith et al., 2019; Souri et al., 2018). The big five questionnaire provides a more reliable measure of personality traits than in-person interviews. This is because when the questions are asked in person, a participant is more likely to include personal bias (Bahcekapili et al., 2020; Barnett et al., 2015; Bawack et al., 2021; Caprara, 1993; Condon, 2017; Daljeet et al., 2017; Usakli, 2019).

After permission was granted by the Institutional Review Board (IRB), the sample population was selected using a purposive sampling technique to achieve saturation (Lambert & Lambert, 2012). While larger samples can produce broader findings, a smaller sample provides a more profound understanding of the phenomenon (Spiers & Riley, 2019). Purposive sampling is a nonparametric strategy that researchers use to recruit participants who share common knowledge, experience, and understanding of a phenomenon (Bloomberg, 2018; Yin, 2016). According to Etikan et al. (2016), purposeful sampling is typically used in qualitative research because it can provide rich information for the case. Therefore, the purposive sampling technique is nonrandom and considered appropriate for selecting participants. This study aimed to recruit consumers who purchased online courses and had firsthand information about the experience and usage, the course characteristics, and the perceived value.

Interviews were scheduled with participants at their convenience within one week of the initial survey. Semi-structured interviews consisted of a detailed interview. On the interview day, an interview protocol utilizing IRB ethical practices was used to conduct the interview. The purpose was to ensure a standard order with interview participants (Lee & Aslam, 2018). The interview secessions lasted 45-60 minutes and consisted of Zoom recordings to record participants after asking permission. Participants' identities were concealed during the interviews, including their responses. Pseudonyms replaced their real identities. While interviewing participants, the researcher took notes on important issues during data analysis, such as identifying possible biases during the interviews (Maxwell, 2012).

Recordings were transcribed and, after member checking, were imported into NVivo 12

Pro. A data review examined themes and patterns related to the study. The collected data was

securely stored on a personal computer using a unique password. The researcher will store all

hard copies in a secure cabinet. Raw data was transcribed immediately to avoid possible data loss

and readiness for data analysis.

Data Collection and Analysis

The data and collection analysis was a inductive thematic analysis approach (Bloor &

Wood, 2006; Williams, 2021). The data analysis included interpreting the data to examine how

emerging themes addressed the research questions through inductive thematic analysis (Belotto,

2021; Braun & Clarke, 2006). Inductive thematic analysis is common in qualitative research

because themes are not predetermined prior to the research. Inductive thematic analysis is a

descriptive method used to determine data patterns (Braun & Clarke, 2006; Castleberry & Nolen,

2018; Rogers, 2018; Sibeoni et al., 2020). It begins with observing a phenomenon (Bamberg,

2021; Braun & Clarke, 2006). Inductive thematic analysis entails coding the data allowing the

data to be collected first, then searching for patterns by attaching codes to units of data. Sibeoni

et al. (2020) used an inductive and phenomenological approach in medical research to

systematically translate the data into practical solutions. Similarly, Wohlfart et al. (2021) used an

inductive approach with TAM theory to study the effects of Covid-19 among teachers and their

acceptance of digital tools.

After the data collection process, the researcher transcribed the interviews before

embarking on inductive thematic analysis. Member checking was performed to ensure credibility

and prevent researcher bias. Member checking and peer debriefing were used to promote the

dependability of the results by providing participants with time to check the accuracy of their narrations before data analysis (Birt et al., 2016). This ensured credibility and eliminated researcher bias (Creswell & Miller, 2000). After transcription, the document was emailed to the participant to approve or suggest edits. Wording included, "Please respond within three business days. Lack of response will acknowledge that all information represents an accurate transcription."

The steps in the inductive thematic data of the transcripts were as follows:

1. The researcher familiarized herself with the data by reading and rereading interview responses to have a detailed knowledge of interview questions and responses (Braun & Clarke, 2006). NVivo 12 Pro software, a common tool used in qualitative research, was used to organize the transcripts for this and all subsequent steps of the inductive thematic analysis (Castleberry & Nolen, 2018).

2. The second step was the iterative coding of the transcripts (Braun & Clarke, 2006). Coding occurred for two consecutive iterations without adding new codes, altering existing codes, or deleting existing ones.

3. The third step was categorizing the codes iteratively (Braun & Clarke, 2006). The decision rule for categorizing two or more codes was that they were related to the same concept from the theoretical framework. Categorizing codes occurred for two consecutive iterations without adding new categories, altering existing categories, or deleting existing ones.

4. The fourth step was iteratively developing the themes from the categories (Braun & Clarke, 2006). This was performed using pattern analysis. When two or more categories of codes moved together positively or negatively, they were combined to

develop a theme. Iterative pattern analysis occurred until two consecutive iterations without adding new themes, altering existing themes, or deleting existing themes.

5. The fifth step was defining and naming the themes (Braun & Clarke, 2006). In this stage, the researcher provided professional names for the themes generated for easier identification and further analysis.

6. In the last step, the researcher extracted direct quotations representative of each code, category, and theme and wrote the final report. The report included the researcher aligning the research findings with existing literature. The identified themes were compared and contrasted against the existing literature to determine how the themes align with existing knowledge on the topic.

Assumptions

Assumptions refer to the researcher's findings to be true in a given study (Cassell et al., 2018; Patton, 2015). There are key assumptions for most research studies. The first assumption of the research is that participants were truthful. Second, it assumes that the selected participants would be knowledgeable on the topic and honest with their responses. This assumption is necessary because obtaining honest responses from participants promoted the study findings' validity, reliability, and trustworthiness.

Assumptions specific to this study included the assumption that the participant had a basic familiarity with a personal computer or similar and the Internet. Next, the chosen sample size assumes sufficiency to represent the required insights about course characteristics and how the consumer perceives the value of the course (Galvin, 2015). Purposeful sampling is a common choice in qualitative studies (Kalu, 2019). Therefore, a purposeful sampling technique used to recruit participants was less biased and was adequate in identifying participants with rich online

purchasing knowledge, particularly in OPK courses (Kalu, 2019; Maxwell, 2012).

Finally, triangulation is a method used to ensure credibility and validity (Creswell &

Miller, 2000; Salkind, 2010; Santos et al., 2020). Using several sources to identify patterns, such

as literature review, data collection, member checking, and existing theories, provides

triangulation that limits threats to credibility and trustworthiness (Creswell & Miller, 2000;

Johnson et al., 2004, Salkind, 2010; Santos et al., 2020). The first step in the triangulation

process was the chapter 2 literature review. The study includes triangulation using literature

analysis, semi-structured interviews, and data collection with consumers who have purchased

online knowledge products from 2018–2021.

Limitations

Limitations are potential weaknesses or flaws in a given study (Theofanidis & Fountouki,

2019). This study has some limitations. The first relates to the sample size. Qualitative studies

use a small sample size to conduct research which can lead to limited scope (Galvin, 2015;

Malterud et al., 2021; Mason, 2010). However, to mitigate this limitation, the researcher ensured

that participants were knowledgeable about the study topic through a purposeful sampling

process.

The second limitation is the data collection process during the interviews. While

interviews help describe rich detail and patterns, researcher bias can affect interpretation of the

results (Etikan et al., 2016; Galletta, 2013). One suggestion to alleviate this limitation would be

to use a Likert Scale. Forcing the interviewees to choose an answer on a six-point scale

eliminates variances. This can eliminate variances that can make the results unclear.

Furthermore, the research should ensure that the data collected will provide detailed, in-depth information. However, as this study examined a phenomenon, allowing the participants to answer freely allowed for rich data to allow themes to emerge.

The third limitation relates to technology. Participants must be able to use Zoom or other applications that allow the participant and the interviewer to see and hear one another; not observing the participant in a physical space limits the researcher's ability to respond to physical and emotional cues (Gray et al., 2020). As this study specifically examined the OPK market, an assumption is that the participant is proficient with fundamental aspects of technology.

Delimitations

Delimitations are a helpful way to set boundaries for the study. For example, this case study represents a snapshot of a particular group of people at a specified time (Esmene, 2021; Sibeoni et al., 2020). The study used location as a delimitation by focusing on OPK courses purchased by U.S. consumers (Theofanidis & Fountouki, 2019). Therefore, the study excludes participants who reside outside of the United States.

The study also delimited the type of OPK purchased. Exclusion includes consumers who buy OPK products other than independent courses (outside college or university). This included products such as audiobooks, music, movies, and games. This delimitation aimed to ensure that the study was aligned with the overreaching objectives and purpose and provided boundaries.

Ethical Assurances

Essential ethical guidelines must guide research using human participants to ensure that they are informed, have given consent, have their privacy protected, and are well treated and protected against potential harm (DiCicco-Bloom et al., 2006; HHS, 2021). The researcher received Northcentral University's Institutional Review Board (IRB) approval before data collection began as a primary requirement. In addition, CITI certification assures an understanding of ethical procedures. The study complied with the ethical guidelines outlined in the Belmont Report. According to the U.S. Department of Health and Human Services (HHS, 2021), the three fundamental principles outlined in the Belmont Report include respect for persons, beneficence, and justice.

Respect for persons informs participants that participation in the study was voluntary. Beneficence demonstrates professional, courteous interactions throughout the process. This particular study had minimal risks compared to the benefits. The purpose of understanding the contextual information of personality traits and OPK course characteristics and exploring how they may impact the consumer's perceived value is to provide in-depth information to the digital content industry and extend literature with minimal risk to the participant. As such, the benefits outweigh the possible risk in the study (Fielding et al., 2017). Equal opportunities to participate in the study account for justice. Further, the recruitment process was free from bias, as no protected or vulnerable groups were singled out (Anabo et al., 2019). Due to the nature and topic of this study, participants likely used social media and the Internet as they purchased online courses. An inclusion criterion was used in recruitment to ensure eligible participants could participate in the study.

The researcher's role in this study was to recruit participants who met the selection criteria and act as the primary data collector. In this case, the researcher collected data using surveys as a demographic qualification and semi-structured interviews from 22 participants and ensured that every research process was well facilitated. Second, the researcher had the role of minimizing the level of bias in a study, as mentioned previously. To achieve this, the researcher fully disclosed the study's interests (Baksh, 2018; Esmene, 2021; Shufutinsky, 2020). Withholding the personal opinions and experiences of the researcher in the OPK market was a relevant strategy to prevent bias in the study. Third, the researcher upholds ethical principles that apply to social research (Hammersley, 2015). For instance, the researcher had the role of ensuring participants' confidentiality and privacy.

Before participating in the study, during the screening process, participants provided an informed consent letter to sign. An informed consent form ensured that participants understood the ethical compliance in this research, including key components related to the Belmont principles, such as voluntary participation and confidentiality. This information was included at the beginning of the Qualtrics survey of personality traits and reviewed again to receive verbal consent before the interview. The informed consent also detailed data storage and avoidance of a potential breach.

All identifying information used a coding system to safeguard participants' confidentiality and privacy. All data will be stored on an external hard drive that is password-protected in accordance with IRB requirements for three years and then destroyed. Printed materials will be stored in a locked filing cabinet and shredded at the end of the 3-year retention period. Lastly, the researcher maintained communication with participants by providing a platform where participants were free to raise concerns about the study.

Summary

Chapter 3 included a discussion of the research methods. First, the introduction included the problem and purpose statement, allowing for precise alignment between the problem statement, purpose, and research design. Next are materials, study procedures, data analysis, assumptions, limitations, delimitations, and ethical assurances concerning this research. The research methodology and design, population, and sample provided information on the research structure, including a Qualtrics personality survey and an interview of people who have purchased OPK courses from 2018–2021. Further, a qualitative method is compatible with the problem statement and purpose in that it provides a better understanding of the phenomena of the OPK market and contributes rich data not found in quantitative analysis (Shufutinsky, 2020). The qualitative research method is best suited for this study as it adds to existing research by exploring TAM in light of new data, such as the OPK market (Willig, 2019).

    The semi-structured interviews provided core information from the participant while also providing the flexibility to note the deeper experiences of different personality types and their perception of relevant factors of the TAM theory. In addition, the semi-structured interviews added new knowledge to the existing limited literature in the OPK course market. The following section is Chapter 4, which presents the study findings.

Chapter 4: Findings

The problem in this study addressed the question of how personality traits of consumers perceive value of OPK products using perceived usefulness (PU) and perceived ease of use (PEOU) as constructs among consumers in the United States (Bahl et al., 2019; Fu et al., 2020; Jin et al., 2020; Jing et al., 2020; Seibert et al., 2021; Su et al., 2019). Su et al. (2019) cited the need for further inquiry to understand how perceived value in the OPK market is affected by personality traits. Similarly, Bahl et al. (2019) and Seibert et al. (2021) expressed a need for further research on more specific technologies related to personality traits rather than technology in general. Several studies have called for further research on the TAM model, including investigating user perspectives in e-learning (Mohammadi, 2015) and further exploration of product characteristics: service quality, information quality, and system quality (Jin, 2020). In a study on knowledge products in China, Fu et al. (2020) suggested future research on knowledge products and consumer satisfaction from other countries. Failure to understand personality traits within the constructs of OPK characteristics as well as their perception of value could result in failed marketing strategies among digital entrepreneurs as competition in the OPK market continues to grow (Beig et al., 2019; Fu et al., 2020; Kraus, 2018; Marbach et al., 2016; Matarazzo, 2021; Su et al., 2019).

The purpose of this qualitative case study was to examine how different personality traits describe value within the constructs of PU and PEOU of online courses in the OPK market using the contextual antecedents of OPK characteristics of consumers in the United States from 2018–2021. Usakli (2019) called for further research on personality traits in online shopping using a qualitative method. They further suggested that studies should be expanded beyond higher education and use participants other than students predominantly in research. Zhou et al. (2022)

suggested that future studies focus on consumer characteristics in electronic commerce.

Understanding consumer's personality traits within the OPK market constructs of OPK product

characteristics helps identify consumer preferences and their PU and PEOU (Barnett, 2015).

The chapter is organized around the research procedures for qualitative analysis outlined

by Braun and Clark (2006). First, trustworthiness, credibility, dependability, and confirmability

are reviewed. Secondly, the results are presented with briefly summarized demographic

information, and the participants' personality characteristics are explained. These characteristics

were used during the pattern analysis from which the themes were derived. The following tabular

illustration is shared with the initial codes, examples, direct quotations, and counts. Tables

present how codes were formed into categories and how these categories were formed into

themes. These tables are discussed based on Braun and Clarke's (2006) procedure for inductive

thematic analysis procedure. Thirdly, the researcher discussed the themes extracted from the data

through this analysis process. Then, a discussion ensues on these same themes and their

association with the research questions. A section describing the evaluation of the findings and a

summary close the chapter.

Trustworthiness of the Data

Credibility, dependability, transferability, and confirmability ensured the trustworthiness

of the qualitative data for the thematic analysis (Castleberry & Nolen, 2018). Credibility entails

the validity of the qualitative data included in the transcripts derived from the semi-structured

interviews (Shenton, 2004; Wood et al., 2020). Trustworthiness is established using Braun and

Clark (2006). Per Braun and Clarke's (2006) guidance for the thematic analysis of qualitative

data, member-checking was used to ensure that the information included in the transcripts was

valid. Each study participant was emailed the full transcript of their respective interviews for this study and informed that they had one business week to respond with revision requests and/or corrections. None of the study participants made such a request.

Dependability in qualitative research is what replicability is in quantitative research (Belotto, 2018). To ensure that other researchers may repeat the study for other contexts and samples, an in-depth description of the methodology (described in detail in chapter 3) allows for future studies to repeat the current research. Specifically, the documentation of study implementation, from screening potential participants for study participation eligibility to recruiting eligible individuals for study participation to gaining informed consent, to data collection, analysis, and management was recorded (Belotto, 2018).

Transferability is the extent to which the results of a study may inform decision-making about other samples in other contexts (Shenton, 2004). Per Shenton (2004), transferability was ensured by a thick description of a sample large enough to demonstrate variation for key concepts of the study. The first subsection of the results section in this chapter includes a description of the study participants' respective genders and personality types.

Confirmability in qualitative research occurs when steps are taken to ensure that the results are not a function of researcher and participant bias (Moon et al., 2016). To ensure confirmability for the researcher, clear decision rules for coding, categorizing codes, and interpreting themes from the categories of codes were articulated (Moon et al., 2006). Moreover, the decision rules for developing and presenting the implications of the results for theory, future research, and practice are articulated at the outset of Chapter 5. To ensure confirmability for the study participants, they were informed that their participation was confidential to reduce the likelihood of social response bias (Moon et al., 2006).

Results

The results are presented as follows. First, demographic information is provided. The

participants are described by personality type and gender. Secondly, the thematic analysis results

are presented per the six steps that Braun and Clarke (2006) specified for the thematic analysis of

qualitative data. An explanation of the decision rules for identifying codes, combining codes into

categories, and interpreting categories into themes by pattern analysis is included at the outset of

each subsection of the thematic analysis subsection. Thirdly, the themes are presented by

salience to the research questions.

Demographic Information

The characteristics of the study participants are detailed in Table 1 below. The table only

includes characteristics for which there is variation across participants. For qualitative data

analysis, participant characteristics demonstrate variations that may aid the pattern analysis that

informs theme development (Braun & Clarke, 2006). The description of the study participants' is

organized by personality type. The pattern analysis of how the personality types mapped to the

different themes from the inductive qualitative analysis of the interview transcripts are reserved

for subsequent sections of this chapter focused on the results of the qualitative data analysis

using NVivo 12 qualitative data analysis software to implement Braun and Clarke's (2006) six

steps for inductive thematic analysis.

Table 1

Study Participants by Gender Identity, Personality

Participant	Gender	Personality type
P1	Female	Agreeableness
P2	Female	Agreeableness
P3	Female	Agreeableness

P4	Female	Agreeableness
P5	Female	Agreeableness
P6	Female	Agreeableness
P7	Female	Agreeableness/Conscientiousness
P8	Female	Agreeableness/Neuroticism
P9	Female	Agreeableness/Openness to Experience
P10	Male	Agreeableness/Extroversion
P11	Female	Conscientiousness
P12	Female	Conscientiousness
P13	Male	Conscientiousness
P14	Female	Conscientiousness/Agreeableness
P15	Male	Extroversion
P16	Female	Extroversion/Agreeableness
P17	Female	Neuroticism
P18	Female	Neuroticism/Agreeableness
P19	Male	Openness to Experience
P20	Female	Openness to Experience
P21	Male	Openness to Experience
P22	Female	Openness to Experience

Participant Personality Types

Establishing personality types was essential to the research problem. Research Question 1 examined how personality trait factors impact customer perceptions of the course characteristics. Research Question 2 also uses the participant's personality traits to discuss the consumer's perceived value. Therefore, an overview of the participants' personality traits proceeds the discussion of themes aligned with the research questions.

Agreeableness.

The predominance of the study participants (77%) identified as female, and 13 participants (59%) had agreeableness as one or more trait. Six of the participant's personality types were only agreeableness (27%). All but one of the participants with the personality type of agreeableness identified as female (95%). Seven of the study participants had the personality type of agreeableness as one of two personality types (31%). Four of these had agreeableness as the primary personality type, with another personality type as a secondary personality type (18%). Three of these study participants identified as female and had secondary personality types of conscientiousness, neuroticism, and openness to experience. The fourth identified as male and has extroversion as the secondary personality type. Three of the study participants had agreeableness as the secondary personality type. These three participants identified as female and had primary personality types of conscientiousness, extroversion, and neuroticism.

Conscientiousness.

Five participants demonstrated conscientiousness as either a sole trait or a combination with other traits (22%). Three study participants had the personality type of conscientiousness. Two of these three participants identified as female, and the other identified as male. One study participant who identified as female had conscientiousness as the primary personality type and agreeableness as the secondary personality type. One study participant who identified as female had conscientiousness as a secondary personality type and agreeableness as the primary personality type. The single study participant with agreeableness as any part of his personality had agreeableness as the primary personality type and extroversion as the secondary personality type.

Extroversion.

Three study participants had extroversion as the personality type (13%). Of these, one identified as female, and two identified as male. One study participant identifying as female had extroversion as the primary personality type and agreeableness as the secondary personality type. One study participant identifying as male had agreeableness as the primary personality type and extroversion as the secondary personality type. Another participant identified as a male and had extroversion as the sole trait.

Neuroticism.

Three study participants had neuroticism as at least part of their respective personality

types (13%). The study participant with neuroticism as the only personality type identified as

female. One study participant who identified as female had neuroticism as the primary

personality type and agreeableness as the secondary personality type. One study participant who

identified as female had neuroticism as the secondary personality type and agreeableness as the

secondary primary type. No study participants identifying as male had neuroticism as a

personality type.

Openness to Experience.

Four of the study participants had openness to experience as the personality type (18%).

The study participant with neuroticism as the only personality type identified as female. One

study participant who identified as female had agreeableness as the primary personality type and

openness to experience as the secondary personality type.

Steps Taken to Analyze the Data

A total of 22 interviews were completed with consumers of OPK courses. The process of

thematic analysis was completed using NVivo 12, a qualitative organizational software that aids

in developing thematic analysis results. The researcher followed Braun and Clarke's (2006)

thematic analysis procedures to complete the coding procedures for this dissertation.

Inductive Thematic Analysis, Steps 1 and 2: Coding Procedures and Development

Following the recommendations of Braun and Clarke (2006), the first step of inductive

thematic analysis procedures was to become familiarized with the textual information. For this

purpose, the textual data was read and re-read, a total of three iterations, to ensure a thorough

understanding and familiarization with the textual data derived from the participants for the study. Proceeding with this step, the researcher initiated the coding procedures discussed in this section.

The coding procedures initiated with assessing content for repeated textual information across the 22 interviews. The researcher examined the textual data by assessing for repeated phrases, words, or concepts of similar value (Braun & Clarke, 2006). A total of three rounds of coding procedures were completed to assess for missed information. The researcher completed coding procedures until no new information was identified following the first phase of Braun and Clarke (2006) for inductive thematic analysis. After three rounds of code identification, a total of 19 codes were developed based on the resultant interviews completed with participants for the study. Table 2 demonstrates these codes, descriptions, quotes, participant count, and frequency tallies. Participant count is the count of participants with at least one direct quotation associated with a focal code. Frequency count is the count of direct quotations associated with a focal code.

Table 2

Codes, Examples, Direct Quotations, and Counts

Code label	Example direct quotation	Participant count	Frequency count
Accountability	P1: "I wish they would have kept it the old way where it was someone there keeping you accountable....."	8	45
Added Value	P9: "It definitely added to the value for sure, and I've been coaching ever since, and I'm definitely using the content regularly."	10	85
Benefit(s)	P3: "Well, one thing that was a benefit to me is that it really did give you tools where you can get around to thinking like an online retailer.	15	16
Course Characteristics	P20: "There were 12 components. Some weeks we covered multiple components. Other weeks, we just covered one aspect of it."	17	20
Credibility	P16: "Well, it was a professor for one, and one who had the experience, had a doctorate, had a practice, so I felt like this person knew the subject matter. But, for the value, I would have liked to have had more."	11	22
Dislike(s)	P7: "It was like you showed up for the live course, and they're going to talk about section 2 or whatever, so then they do it live, and then if you have to get the replay later if you're not there live."	9	23
Ease	P19: "So it was that initial prettiness. But then, in the long term, it was not as useful as something like Kajabi. That doesn't look as pretty, but the organization is just so functional."	20	45

Code label	Example direct quotation	Participant count	Frequency count
Engagement	P2: "I feel like I'm more engaged if it's live online."	16	78
Information Gain	P8: "I believe the value of just getting general knowledge from these courses will help me decide whether I want to pursue that more."	20	96
Instructor competency	P5: "My instructor in there was. She knew what she was doing mostly, but she didn't explain it well. She was cold. I just did not connect with her. I didn't learn well with her."	12	63
Online Course Experience	P4: "I've done quite a few, actually, and I've had a good experience with them. Let's say I've done. I mean three main ones or no one, three big ones, like where it was like, you know, for an extended period of time."	18	12
Pace	P14: "I like that I can do it at my own pace and look for the course that I need depending on what I'm working on at the time."	12	45
Personal Interests	P18: "I think it just depends on the person. Like I loved college, but college would have been very difficult for me to go to as a stay-at-home mom."	17	24
Platform(s)	P9: "I had a couple of issues just with Zoom, right? Like platform type things a few times when we would do coaching, and then it'd be glitching or something going on would be external, I guess, obstacle."	15	35
Personality	P11: "I know how to work. I know how to structure myself. I have, like, I know how to do four things at once. I know how to focus in and get this project done without worrying about their project over there."	20	56

Code label	Example direct quotation	Participant count	Frequency count
Quality	P4: "The quality did give me pause. It was a little bit difficult to navigate, kind of hard to find exactly what I wanted.	19	89
Service	P22: "The customer service was phenomenal. I had lots of questions and what happens if I miss a week and what happens if that time doesn't work?"	13	45
Usefulness	P19: "...[I] just love how many opportunities there are for people to make money and create businesses and help other people with these online courses, and you can reach anyone across the world, really."	11	12
Lack of Value	P20: "I don't think the course is what's valuable. I think the result that you get in relation to the time and the effort to get to that result, versus or divided by the experience you were experiencing in the wall you were hitting before, is what makes the course valuable, not the actual course itself."	8	19

Codes included phrases of similar value, such as *instructor, pace,* and *engagement.* For example, P2 said, "I feel like I'm more engaged if it's live online." For the code *information gained,* P8 reflected, "I believe the value of just getting general knowledge from these courses helps me decide whether I want to pursue that more." Furthermore, P5, in terms of instructor competency, "My instructor mostly knew what she was doing, but she did not explain it well. She was cold. I just did not connect with her. I didn't learn well with her." These phrases and statements led to the development of 19 total codes. The decision rule was to ensure a total of two iterations of coding procedures to prevent any missed information and ensure all phrases, words, and sentences of relevant or similar value were coded. The developed codes demonstrated

a variety of experiences ranging from personality factors, ease, usefulness, and features related to

OPK characteristics and platforms. The developed codes, derived from the recommendations of

Braun and Clarke (2006), phases one and two of inductive thematic analysis laid the foundation

for categorization procedures, discussed next.

Inductive Thematic Analysis, Step 3: Category Development

Table 3

From Codes to Categories

Category	Codes (from Table 2)	Definition	Participant count	Frequency count
Personality Factors	Personality Personal Interests	Participant personality factors were relevant to their interests in engaging with OPK as well as how they perceived the value of the product.	22	80
OPK Characteristics	Quality Service	Participants reflected on differing experiences with quality and service usage among OPK products. Service and quality were often dictated by the organization of material if platforms supplied additional tools and how information was delivered.	22	134
Perceived Usefulness (PU)	Usefulness Information Gained	The perceived usefulness of products was based on individuals' ability to gain information that was considered applicable to their own needs or goals. The usefulness of the	22	108

Category	Codes (from Table 2)	Definition	Participant count	Frequency count
		product was also based on the information that was supplied by the service.		
Perceived Ease of Use (PEOU)	Ease	Participants perceived ease of use varied by each individual based on course characteristics and ease of use. The ease of the product, combined with various tools and means of information delivery, was crucial to participants' perceptions of perceived ease of use.	22	65
	Course Characteristics			
Use of OPK	Pace	The use of OPK was dictated, in part, for participants in considering how products were useful and easy to use based on pacing, engagement, and benefits of the product to themselves, which were crucial to their adaption of the products.	22	139
	Benefit(s)			
	Engagement			
Value of OPK	Added Value	The value of OPK products was discussed by participants in terms of their experience (present and past) with online courses, the value added (by themselves or the course), and the inherent value of the product. Participants emphasized the importance of gaining value from the information based on motivation, goal obtainment, and ability to apply information to their own needs.	22	116
	Online Course Experience			
	Value			
Platform Characteristics			22	98
	Instructor			
	Platform(s)			

Category	Codes (from Table 2)	Definition	Participant count	Frequency count
Challenges of OPK	Accountability Credibility Dislike(s)	Participants discussed the importance of an engaging and empathetic instructor. The platform tools, usability, and access were also important characteristics that aided in the participants' overall perception of the OPK product and applicability for their own purposes. Participants' applicability of OPK was also dictated by challenges experienced. The dislikes varied individually but often centered upon the platform tools, lack of credibility, and difficulty with lacking accountability in some OPK products. These factors influenced their usage of products.	22	90

The developed eight categories referenced concepts such as *challenges of OPK, platform characteristics*, and *use of OPK*. The categories developed illustrated the variations in individual PU and PEOU based on participants' experiences, challenges, and perceived benefits of OPK products. Participants also discussed the difficulty in using OPK products based on factors such as engagement, accountability, and credibility of the platform and instructors. For example, *perceived ease of use (PEOU)* referenced the codes of *ease* and *course characteristics*. P14 noted, "I think the basic language was a little basic." And P3, "I had it up and running within 5 minutes. I mean, actually, the only reason it took that long is because just me being distracted with other things."

In terms of categories of *OPK challenges,* P20 stated that "For the most part, it's pretty good if you start a class, you need to bookmark it because it's hard to go back and find it sometimes." And P9, "It's been my experience that you buy in, they give you what they tell you. Whether they give that to you at the highest quality or not." Participants' reflections in the identified eight categories illustrated the difficulty in accessing platforms, benefits as perceived individually, and factors associated with value, added value, and quality and service. Based upon these categories, the researcher-initiated steps four and five of Braun and Clarke's (2006) procedures for theme identification.

Inductive Thematic Analysis, Steps 4 and 5: Themes

The fourth and fifth steps of Braun and Clarke's (2006) process of inductive thematic analysis combined categories into themes. For this process, three iterations of thematic analysis were completed. The decision rule for developing themes for this dissertation was based on the recommendations of Braun and Clarke (2006). A minimum of two categories were included within each theme holding relevant value or conceptual data. A total of four final themes were identified, which are exemplified in Table 4. The themes, categories, definitions, participant count, and frequency count related to the textual data are also reviewed in Table 4.

Table 4

From Categories to Themes

Theme	Categories (from Table 3)	Definition	Participant count	Frequency count
Personality Factors via OPK Characteristics	Personality Factors OPK Characteristics	Participants' personality factors reflected varied usage of OPK products based on the characteristics of the platforms. The participant's variation in personality types (agreeableness, openness, neuroticism, conscientiousness, and extroversion) were important factors in terms of how the characteristics of the platforms were used and perceived by participants.	22	214
Perceived Ease of Use via Platform Characteristics	Perceived Ease of Use Platform Characteristics	The ease of use for OPK Products was influenced by the platform characteristics. Each platform offered differing formats for learning which were important factors in participants' understanding of the ease of use of OPK products.	22	163
Perceived Usefulness via Value of OPK	Perceived Usefulness Value of OPK	Participants' perception of OPK value influenced the perceived usefulness of OPK products. The value of OPK was unique for each participant's goals, platform usage, and understanding of information value, which was key in their definition of the	22	224

Theme	Categories (from Table 3)	Definition	Participant count	Frequency count
		perceived usefulness of OPK Products.		
Use of OPK via Challenges of OPK	Use of OPK Challenges of OPK	Participants emphasized that using OPK was dictated by personal factors such as previous use of online products, the pace, engagement, and perceived benefits. In turn, the challenges of OPK, such as credibility, dislikes, and accountability, were influential in participants' final use of an OPK product.	22	229

The final developed themes included *personality factors via OPK characteristics, perceived ease of use (PEOU) via platform characteristics, perceived usefulness (PU) by a value of OPK, and use of OPK via challenges of OPK.* Following the delineated decision rule, a minimum of two categories were included within each theme to ensure the relevancy of similar values or concepts. For example, *perceived usefulness (PU) via the value of OPK* consisted of the categories of *perceived usefulness (PU)* and *value of OPK.* The first theme, *personality factors by OPK characteristics*, consisted of the categories of *personality factors* and *OPK characteristics.* In the proceeding sections of Chapter 4, the researcher presents each of these themes and relevant participant quotes.

Resultant Themes from the Analysis

The final developed themes included *personality factors via OPK characteristics, perceived ease of use (PEOU) via platform characteristics, perceived usefulness (PU) by a value of OPK, and use of OPK via challenges of OPK*, all of which align with research questions 1 and 2. Following the delineated decision rule, a minimum of two categories were included within each theme to ensure the relevancy of similar values or concepts. For example, *perceived usefulness (PU) via the value of OPK* consisted of the categories of *perceived usefulness (PU)* and *value of OPK*. The first theme, *personality factors by OPK characteristics*, consisted of the categories of *personality factors* and *OPK characteristics*. In the proceeding sections of Chapter 4, the researcher presents each of these themes and relevant participant quotes.

RQ1 - Theme 1: Personality Factors via OPK Characteristics

The first theme, *personality factors via OPK characteristics*, was created by combining the categories of *personality factors* and *OPK characteristics*. Figure 1 demonstrates the relationship between codes, categories, and the development of theme one.

Figure 1

Theme One: Personality Factors via OPK Characteristics

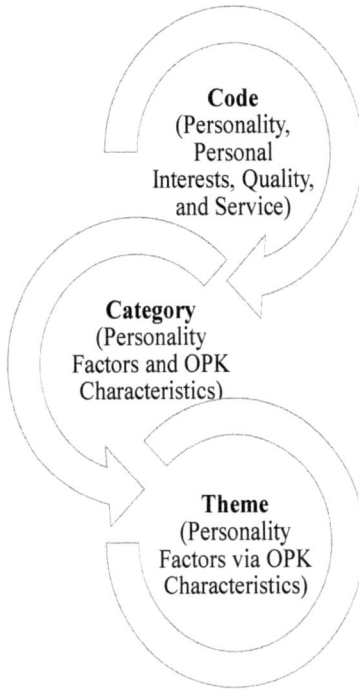

Code
(Personality,
Personal
Interests, Quality,
and Service)

Category
(Personality
Factors and OPK
Characteristics)

Theme
(Personality
Factors via OPK
Characteristics)

Participants in Theme 1 discussed various personal preferences toward learning and

platform characteristics. Participants reviewed the importance of platform characteristics that

influence the perception of OPK and the use of these products for personal knowledge gain.

Participants also discussed the importance of quality and service in relationship with OPK usage

and knowledge. In terms of quality, P1 said, "I've never had really any issues. To me, they're

pretty streamlined." and P3 said, "As soon as you signed up, you got access, you got your login, et cetera, et cetera, and the communication was super good." Also, P13, "Very user-friendly and very easy to manage. No problems." P12, referencing service, stated:

> I can watch the videos and learn and go away from it, you know, do 10 minutes a day. That's fun. But when you're having to write and write and write for an hour, and you know you've got to turn this in for an assignment, it's not as enjoyable.

Also, P10 claimed:

> I guess it just made it easier, like when the quality of service, and maybe it has to do with, you know, if there's someone there to answer questions, or if you can't find something, someone's there to tell you oh, you just look in this area of the program to find that answer or find that area of whatever you're looking for.

P20, discussing personal preferences, stated, "I guess it's geared toward my interests versus what I have to do to meet a certain list of criteria for a degree." And P1, "I think it just depends on the person. Like I loved college, but college would have been very difficult for me to go to as a stay-at-home mom." While P4 argued, "I think the rest of them that I have taken have been very simple, clear explanations of everything, the steps were clear, the language was clear." And P15 "I know how to structure myself. I know how to do four things at once. I know how to focus in and get this project done without worrying about their project over there."

Service and connection were important to participants. P2 said, "I probably would go into my own personal history because I think if you're going to connect with people, you have to understand that each and every individual has a story." However, P2 stated:

> What I didn't like about it is this, the complete and utter disregard for how it felt to be the participant on the end of it. And it might have been the most incredible information, but the person that was facilitating the online program, he would speak so low, and he would

speak so low, and he would speak so low, and you'd have to, like, turn the volume up just to hear him, and then and then he'd cough really loudly.

Participants' discussions reflected in theme one illustrated the unique experiences, concerns, and benefits as perceived by users of OPK platforms. The individual perceptions supplied a renewed understanding regarding how differing perceptions, individual personalities, and characteristics of the platforms may influence the use and perception of OPK value.

Consistent with this theme's emphasis on a wide variety of personality factors demonstrating patterns with OPK characteristics, there were clear patterns between participants' big five personality types and theme 1. Figure 2 summarizes the different personality types of the participants whose direct quotations were associated with codes that ultimately were associated with theme 1 via the categories of *personality variation* and *OPK characteristics*.

Figure 2

Theme One by Personality Type, Participant Count

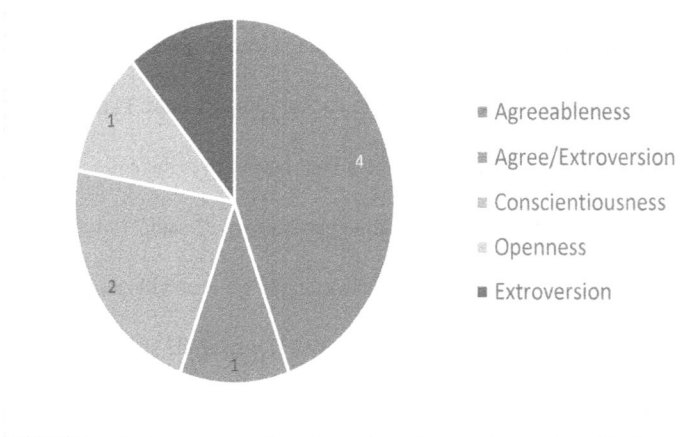

More specifically, four of the study participants associated with the theme had agreeableness as the personality type. One of the study participants associated with theme 1 has agreeableness as the primary personality type and extroversion as the secondary personality type. Two of the study participants associated with theme 1 had conscientiousness as the personality type. One of the study participants associated with theme 1 had openness as the personality type. One of the study participants associated with theme 1 had extroversion as the personality type.

RQ 2 - Theme 2: Perceived Ease of Use (PEOU) via Platform Characteristics

Data from the second theme covered the topics of *perceived ease of use via platform characteristics.* The second theme, *perceived ease of use (PEOU) via platform characteristics,* was developed by combining the categories of *perceived ease of use* (PEOU) and *platform characteristics.* Figure 3 demonstrates the relationship between codes, categories, and the resultant development of these two.

Figure 3

Theme Two: Perceived Ease of Use (PEOU) via Platform Characteristics

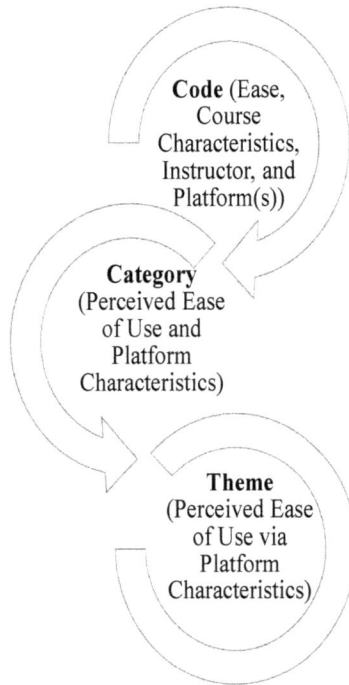

Theme two was derived through a combination of the codes *ease, course characteristics, instructor*, and *platform*. The categories of perceived *ease of use (PEOU)* and *platform characteristics* resulted in the second theme. Data specific to the second theme discussed the ease of use of OPK products as perceived by participants. Participants reflected on different characteristics of platforms, benefits, and instructors, as well as relevant contextual antecedents that aided in their perception of ease of use for OPK products and platforms. For example, in reference to the platforms, P2 said, "I think the basic language was a little basic, it could have been something anyone would have taken, but I felt like it was something I could have seen on the TV." And P3, "I thought it was very equipping and easily applicable." Similarly, P13 stated difficulty in using one course "...the iPhone course, I would more have to go out and do exactly what they were doing rather than it applying to what I wanted to do."

Participants also discussed the useful characteristics of the platform, such as P2, "A lot of the feedback was just from other peers and what they thought." Also, P2, in reference to the instructor, "...[she] comes up very confident, like she knows what she's talking about, and she sells a good product. She sells herself really well. That definitely helps build your belief in her and what she's selling." However, in some cases, the platform was challenging for users, such as P5:

> I mean, it was a lot of repeats of information, and I was like, yeah, I remember learning about that before, you know. And so, it was easy because I listened to it in my car on my way to and from work. So, I would say my interest probably was not; I wasn't focusing as much as I should have been.

Other users felt that there was a need for instructor improvement, such as P5, "I probably would do different reminders, more fun." Also, P2 explained, "It just reminds me a little bit of a podcast, so it reminds me of something I would look at in Spotify." And P1 elaborated:

> I feel like it was a little bit of a circus. You know, meaning, where they offered you so much, and it was so wonderful, but you didn't know which lollipop to grab. You know, and I'm just one person. I just, there's only so many hours in the day, and I needed.

Other users felt that ease of use was lacking in their experience, such as P4:

> I felt overwhelmed, and I think on some level, this may sound weird is, yeah, there was such a jump in trying to grasp all the things they were saying, and I didn't need you don't need everything all at once.

Teacher style was fundamental in some participants' perception of ease of use, such as P7, "...teaching style, I guess just, they're trying to be as interactive as they can." Or P6, "My instructor in there was, she knew what she was doing mostly, but she didn't explain it well. She was cold. I just did not connect with her. I didn't learn well with her." Also, others felt that the platform made a difference in ease of use, such as P11, "I think the app was a little bit more reliable." and P12, "I've never had any issues. To me, they're pretty streamlined." While some faced issues with platforms such as Zoom, like P14, "I had a couple of issues just with Zoom, right? Like platform-type things a few times when we would do coaching, and then it'd be glitching."

Data from theme two supplied unique information from participants regarding their perceived ease of use towards OPK products. The information obtained from participants in this dissertation allowed for a renewed understanding regarding how platform characteristics, such as instructor, and the platform itself, can aid or deter participants perceived ease of use. In Chapter 5, further information is supplied regarding recommendations for research and practice based on the information garnered from theme two.

There was a clear pattern between participants' big five personality types and theme 2. Figure 4 summarizes the different personality types of the participants whose direct quotations were associated with codes that ultimately were associated with theme 2 via the categories of *perceived ease of use (PEOU)* and *platform characteristics*. Each participant associated with theme 2 had agreeableness, conscientiousness, or both personality types.

Figure 4

Theme Two by Personality Type, Participant Count

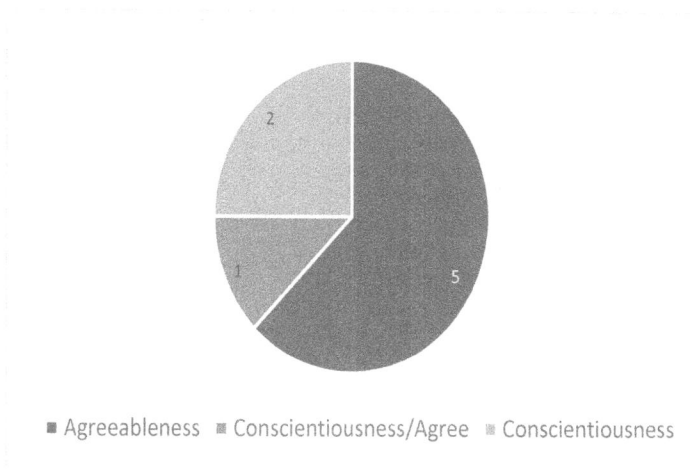

■ Agreeableness ■ Conscientiousness/Agree ■ Conscientiousness

More specifically, five of the study participants associated with the theme had agreeableness as the personality type. Two study participants associated with theme 2 have conscientiousness as the personality type. One of the study participants associated with theme 2 had agreeableness as the primary personality type and conscientiousness as the secondary personality type.

RQ 2 - Theme 3: Perceived Usefulness (PU) via Value Of OPK

The third theme, *perceived usefulness (PU) via the value of OPK*, was derived from the combination of categories of *perceived usefulness* (PU) and the *value of OPK*. Participants in this theme reflected upon their perception of usefulness by considering the value of OPK to themselves, knowledge gained, and added value based upon experiences with online knowledge products. Figure 5 illustrates the relationship between codes and categories that were added to theme three.

Figure 5

Theme Three: Perceived Usefulness (PU) via Value of OPK

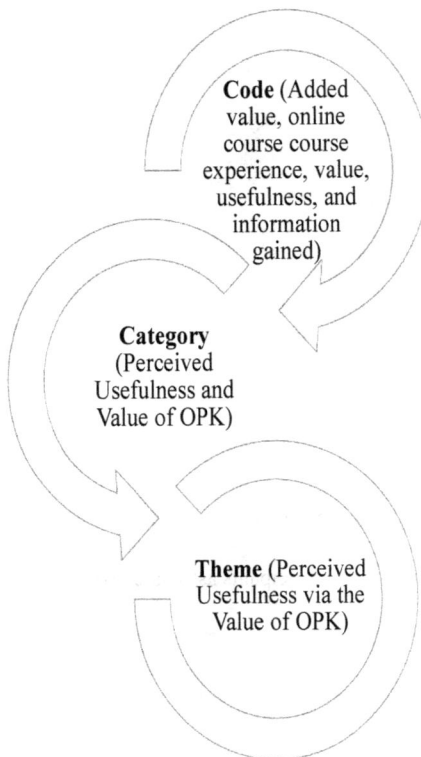

Information from this theme supplied unique data revealing participants' PU of OPK

products. Participants reflected on numerous factors that contributed to their understanding of the

usefulness of OPK products. Additionally, participants discuss added value, value, experiences

with previous products, as well as usefulness in terms of information gained. Participant 11

discussed value: "I believe the value of just getting general knowledge from these courses will

help me decide whether I want to pursue that more." While P3 stated, "I always tended to

complete them. I'm not one to just completely skip something that I've paid for." Also, P1 stated,

"She'd [the educator] had gotten the training, and she presented it in a way that made sense and worked for us."

The value of courses was also based on the ability to use the platform effectively, such as P19's quote:

> I had to call, I wasn't able to get into my classes a few times, and I thought, I'm paying a lot of money to go three days without having access to my courses now. They responded quickly, and they were working on the problem, but I would definitely say the app was better, was more better.

Others perceived value was based on the ability to use the material later, such as P1, "Often you have to go back and remember all that is available to utilize it. So, I think it's mostly in content." And P10, "I think they're great to learn and gain knowledge without having to drive somewhere and use extra time signing up and committing."

The value of products was also based on if personal interests were present for a participant, such as P11, "As long as I could simplify something, it didn't matter, as long as I was able to learn it and it was simplified; it became very useful." Otherwise, P12 felt that the platform's effort was key to usefulness "A lot of thought and planning behind them. You could tell. So, I think the seller, you know, putting in that time and effort was probably what made it really enjoyable and easy." While P18 stated:

> The ones I've taken, and I feel like it's more valuable, like I said, I'll get something in the mail instead of just like, here's the eBook or download this or you know, here's some work with pages or something, something like you actually get the hard paper copy in the mail.

The role of instructors to add value to the course also added value according to P13:

> I would say the communication. It was very easy to get a hold of someone support-wise.
> As part of that course, you got like a bonus login with this whole library of information,
> so it felt like you were getting a lot of those bonus-type items. The material you could
> print out was an added bonus.

Value added was also important to P7, "Having those open office hours are amazing where you can go in, and you have access 9-6 through the day."

The cost of the product and the expected value were unique for each participant, such as P7, "Because it was less than 20 dollars, I felt perfectly fine spending it and actually expected it to be more glitchy than it was." Also, in P17, "I know that part of the low cost was to get you to buy more, and that's fine." A lower price was also a high-value product that was usable for some participants, such as P12, "The presenter was very professional and knew what he was doing. That was not what I was expecting for the price. I was expecting it not to be a professional person." For some, value and usefulness were based on application, such as P19 "when you apply it in every day, you know, principles..." And P16, "They're very valuable if you take the time to really digest it." While others, such as P17, felt value in the application of knowledge:

> I don't think the course is what's valuable. I think the result that you get in relation to the
> time and the effort to get to that result, versus or divided by the experience you were
> experiencing in the wall you were hitting before, is what makes the course valuable, not
> the actual course itself.

Theme three supplied information that improved research understanding of participants' PU of OPK products through consideration of value. Participants reflected unique definitions of OPK value based on personal experience, OPK platforms, and the ability to use and apply knowledge gained.

The pattern between participants' big five personality types and theme 3 is that all three of the study participants with conscientiousness as the personality type was associated with the theme. Figure 6 summarizes the different personality types of the participants whose direct quotations were associated with codes that ultimately were associated with theme 3 via the categories *perceived usefulness* (PU) and *value of OPK*.

Figure 6

Theme Three by Personality Type, Participant Count

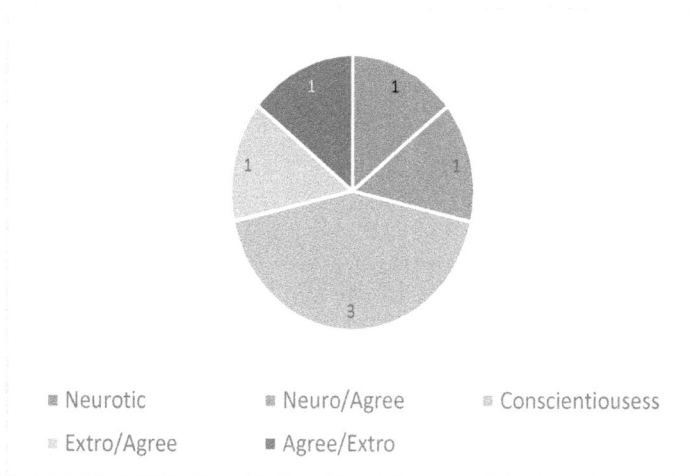

■ Neurotic   ■ Neuro/Agree   ▨ Conscientiousess
▨ Extro/Agree   ■ Agree/Extro

In addition to the three study participants with conscientiousness as the personality type, one of the study participants associated with the theme had neuroticism as the personality type. One of the study participants associated with theme 3 had neuroticism as the primary personality type and agreeableness as the secondary personality type. One of the study participants associated with theme 3 had extroversion as the primary personality type and agreeableness as the secondary personality type. One of the study participants associated with theme 3 had

agreeableness as the primary personality type and extroversion as the secondary personality type.

RQ 1 - Theme 4: Use of OPK via Challenges of OPK

The fourth theme was developed through a combination of categories *use of OPK* and

challenges of OPK. Theme 4, *use of OPK via challenges of OPK*, illustrated the difficulties

participants reported with platforms and the process of knowledge through OPK products.

Additionally, theme 4 illustrates the barriers, and potential factors for improvement, that lead to

individuals' use of OPK. Figure 7 demonstrates codes, categories, and themes relevant to the

development of theme four.

Figure 7

Theme Four: Use of OPK via Challenges of OPK

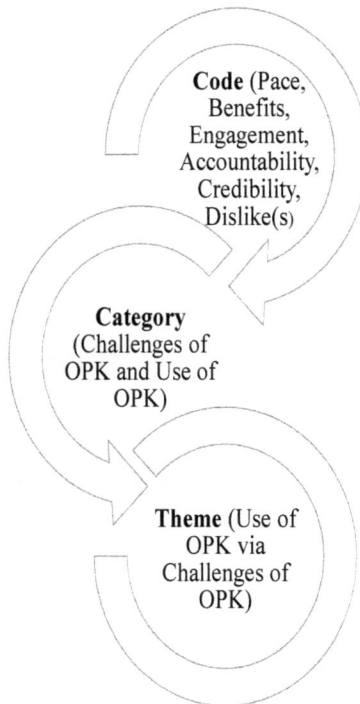

Participants' reflections that led to the development of the fourth theme illustrated potential factors that inhibit or encourage individuals' use of OPK products. Participants discussed factors such as benefits, engagement, pace, accountability, and credibility. The reflections of individuals within this theme demonstrated the complexity of OPK product usage and potential opportunities for platform improvement. For example, in terms of accountability, P6 reported, "I think there's probably a lacking of accountability on some of these that are at your own pace. Sometimes things feel really good to sign up for at the moment, but then everything's like on me to get done, and that can be challenging for me personally." And P3:

I would just make sure that they don't waste their money like I did. You know, if they buy the course, commit to doing it. If it doesn't have a live accountability component to it, maybe doing it with another person, seeing if you can both buy it together and creating that in-person discussion and accountability. If you struggle with that, would be, you know, some advice that I would have for some people.

Others reflected on challenges with the platform course, such as P8, "They never did a good job of explaining. I wish they would have kept it the old way where it was someone there keeping you accountable." The credibility of instructors was also key such as P12 emphasized:

It was a professor for one, and one who had the experience, a doctorate, and a practice, so I felt like this person knew the subject matter. But, for the value, I would have liked to have had more "This is what I experienced in my practice." You know, not necessarily talk about individuals particularly, but have examples of interactions.

P1 felt that the credibility of the platforms and potential educators was lacking: "I kind of felt like I could do what he did after watching him do it one time." And P12 expressed concerns with the credibility of OPK products as well:

I see some of these online courses as snake oil too. So, you know, just selling people a

dream that either is really too hard to attain or people just don't know, don't have the

gumption to actually get to it. I don't know. I mean, it's, you know, just several factors, so

I don't know, it's tricky. I mean, I'm not sure I want to give up that belief in college, but I

absolutely, I mean, even though I say it's snake oil, there are skills that are taught in these

courses that I do think are practical and that you could apply and make some money with

too.

Others expressed dislikes with how information was presented in a less than engaging manner

which affected the use of OPK, such as P13, "What's the benefit of what you're saying? It doesn't

even really make sense, and we're just taking pictures down an alley. I wasn't following it." And

P17, "I just lost interest." Also, P18, "When you sign up for it, like at that moment when they

catch you on Instagram, you're like, Yeah, let's do it. It's free, or it's $7.00 or something like that,

but then life happens."

P20 felt that engagement and platform benefits were crucial reasons for their use of OPK

and online learning knowledge "I would fully engage because if I had a question, I could ask it

right then and there..." Also, P15, "I feel like I'm more engaged if it's live online." Or P6, "I like

live. I am personally okay with either one. I'm not somebody who, when something is live, I'm

not always like engaging in the chat or that sort of thing." The content of the courses was also

important to later use, such as P8:

So, the cheaper courses that I bought didn't come with any type of service, right? There

was no way for me to reach out to somebody and ask a question like, hey, in this video,

you said this, and you know, it's not in the app or whatever it is. And I kind of expected

that going in, right? I don't expect anybody if they're selling a $30.00 course. I liked that it had a live mentor because it created more accountability, and she would give weekly

assignments, and then we had to check back in with her.

P1 said, "I liked that the content in the mentoring class was focused on me and what I needed

and that she customized it." With P13, "I like that I can do it at my own pace and look for the

course that I need depending on what I'm working on at the time. At the same time, I don't

always get to finish the class because things come up, and there's no accountability, so it doesn't

matter if I finish or not."

Data derived from theme 4 demonstrated the challenges that some participants faced with

platforms. Additionally, information derived from participants discussed usage, needed

improvements, and characteristics that improved engagement and led to continued use of OPK

products.

The pattern between participants' big five personality types and theme 4 is that all but

one of the study participants associated with the theme had agreeableness and/or neuroticism

associated with their respective personality types. However, a tandem theme is that the study

participants associated with theme 4 did not have agreeableness and/or neuroticism as their

personality types had conscientiousness as the personality type. Figure 8 summarizes the

different personality types of the participants whose direct quotations were associated with codes

that ultimately were associated with theme 4 via the category's *challenges of OPK* and the *use of*

OPK.

Figure 8

Theme Four by Personality Type, Participant Count

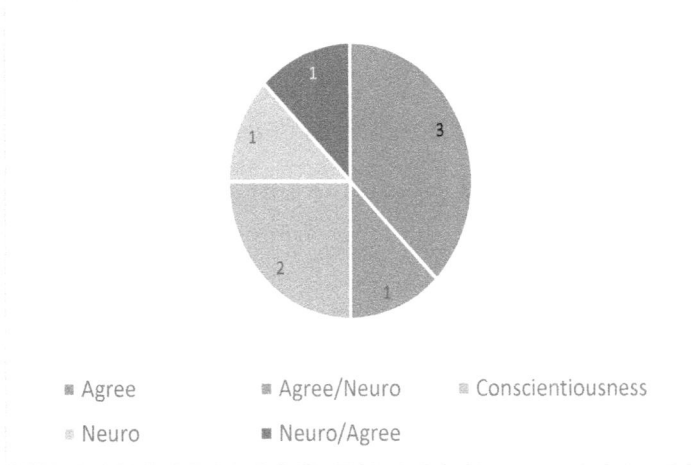

      ◾ Agree   ◾ Agree/Neuro   ◾ Conscientiousness

      ◾ Neuro   ◾ Neuro/Agree

Specifically, three of the study participants associated with the theme had agreeableness as the personality type. One of the study participants associated with theme 4 had agreeableness as the primary personality type and neuroticism as the secondary personality type. One of the study participants associated with theme 4 had neuroticism as the primary personality type and agreeableness as the secondary personality type. One of the study participants associated with theme 4 had neuroticism as the personality type. Two of the study participants associated with theme 4 had conscientiousness as the personality type.

Evaluation of Findings

The final step of Braun and Clark's (2006) thematic analysis procedures for qualitative analysis includes evaluating the findings. The inductive thematic analysis results were mixed vis-à-vis the theories that comprised the theoretical framework that guided data collection and analysis. The next evaluation of the findings is organized by research questions. This evaluation

of the themes vis-à-vis TAM and FFM is driven by whether or not the pattern analysis with

which each theme was developed supported or did not support the propositions of the TAM and

FFM. Accordingly, this evaluation of the findings is a binary exercise. In contrast, discussion of

the patterns underlying the themes that represent developmental contributions to the TAM and/or

the FFM is reserved for the "implications" discussion in Chapter 5.

Research Question 1 and Research Question 2 Aligned by Theme

Table 5 illustrates the themes directly associated with answering the research questions.

Themes 1 and 4 are considered responsive to Research Question 1. Themes 2 and 3 answer

Research Question 2. Note that in an effort to support transferability, the themes were not

renumbered when connected to the research questions. Keeping consistent with the themes as

they emerged allowed for better study procedure replication.

Table 5

Research Questions by Theme

Research question	Theme(s)
RQ1. How do the five personality trait factors (agreeableness, openness, neuroticism, conscientiousness, extroversion) impact consumer perception of online course characteristics (system quality, information quality, service quality)?	Theme 1. Personality Factors vis-a-vis OPK Characteristics Theme 4. Use of OPK vis-a-vis Challenges of OPK
R Q2. How do the five personality trait factors (agreeableness, openness, neuroticism, conscientiousness, extroversion) and the online course characteristics (system quality, information quality, service quality) affect consumer perceived value using the constructs of perceived usefulness (PU) and perceived ease of use (PEOU)?	Theme 2. Perceived Ease of Use (PEOU) vis-a-vis OPK Characteristics Theme 3. Perceived Usefulness (PU) vis-a-vis Value of OPK

Research Question 1: Evaluation of the Findings

Themes 1 and 4 included concepts from both the TAM and the FFM. Tables 6 and 7 present the concepts from both components of the theoretical framework for theme 1 and theme 4, respectively. The decision rule that the association of concepts from the TAM or FFM does not lead to a theme supporting one or both models of the theoretical framework. Instead, the patterns among the TAM and FFM concepts must be similar to what these conceptual models posit. Also, note that the evaluation of the findings in this section does not draw conclusions or address the extent to which the themes represent potentially new developments for the TAM and FFM. These are discussed in Chapter 5.

Table 6

Shared Concepts: Research Question 1 and Theme 1

Research question 1 concepts	Theme 1 concepts	Concepts not shared
FFM: agreeableness, openness, neuroticism, conscientiousness, extroversion TAM: system quality, information quality, service quality	FFM: agreeableness, openness, conscientiousness, extroversion TAM: system quality, information quality, service quality	FFM: neuroticism TAM: none (all are shared)

Table 7

Shared Concepts: Research Question 1 and Theme 4

Research question 1 concepts	Theme 1 concepts	Concepts not shared
FFM: agreeableness, openness, neuroticism, conscientiousness, extroversion TAM: use, perceived difficulty of use	FFM: agreeableness, neuroticism, conscientiousness TAM: use, perceived difficulty of use	FFM: openness, extroversion TAM: none (all are shared)

Theme 1 Supports the TAM and the FFM; Theme 4 Does Not.

The patterns amongst the concepts for the first theme support both the TAM and the FFM. This is not due to the association with most concepts from both conceptual models with the theme but rather with the patterns demonstrated among those concepts. Specifically, the personality types of agreeableness and openness coincided with perceptions of OPK system quality, information quality, and service quality. Because the agreeableness and openness personality types tend to see positive attributes in a focal object (be it a new technology or a person or something else altogether), the coincidence of these personality types with perceptions of OPK quality across all three types of quality is supportive of the FFM (Bandera et al., 2020; Devaraj et al., 2008; Gvili et al., 2019; Harb & Alhayajneh, 2019; Marbach et al., 2016; Prasetya et al., 2015). Moreover, the positive pattern across all three types of OPK quality supports the proposition of the TAM that perceptions of different types of quality beget one another (Ajibade, 2018; Davis, 1989; Yu et al., 2005).

In contrast, the theme 4 patterns among the concepts of the TAM and the FFM are not extensively supportive of either conceptual model included in the theoretical framework. First, the positive pattern of perceived challenges to using OPK and the ease of use OPK are counter to the TAM's proposition that perceived difficulty of use decreases intention to use and actual use, *ceteris paribus* (Ajibade, 2018; Davis, 1989; Yu et al., 2005). Moreover, the positive pattern amongst the personality type neuroticism with both perceived challenges of use and actual use of OPK is counter to the fundamental proposition of the FFM that persons with neurotic personalities are less likely to take risks (Bandera et al., 2020; Devaraj et al., 2008; Gvili et al., 2019; Harb & Alhayajneh, 2019; Marbach et al., 2016; Prasetya et al., 2015). However, the positive pattern of the personality type conscientiousness with perceived challenges of use and actual use supports the FFM proposition that conscientious persons are more likely to engage in sociotechnical scenarios that require thoughtfulness and patience (Ajibade, 2018; Davis, 1989; Yu et al., 2005).

Research Question 2: Evaluation of the Findings

Themes 2 and 3 included concepts from both the TAM and the FFM. Tables 8 and 9 present the concepts from both components of the theoretical framework for theme 2 and theme 3, respectively. The decision rule that the association of concepts from the TAM or FFM does not lead to the conclusion that a theme supports one or both models of the theoretical framework. Instead, the patterns among the TAM and the FFM concepts must be similar to what these conceptual models posit, and past research has supported the models. Also, note that the evaluation of the findings in this section does not address the extent to which the themes represent potentially new developments for the TAM and FFM. Conclusions based on this concept are discussed in Chapter 5.

Table 8

Shared Concepts: Research Question 2 and Theme 2

Research question 2 concepts	Theme 2 concepts	Concepts not shared
FFM: agreeableness, openness, neuroticism, conscientiousness, extroversion TAM: perceived usefulness (PU), perceived ease of use (PEOU)	FFM: agreeableness, conscientiousness TAM: PEOU	FFM: extroversion, openness neuroticism TAM: PU

Table 9

Shared Concepts: Research Question 2 and Theme 3

Research question 2 concepts	Theme 2 concepts	Concepts not shared
FFM: agreeableness, openness, neuroticism, conscientiousness, extroversion TAM: perceived usefulness (PU), perceived ease of use (PEOU)	FFM: agreeableness, neuroticism, conscientiousness, extroversion TAM: PU	FFM: openness TAM: PEOU

Theme 2 Supports the TAM and the FFM; Theme 3 Does Not.

The patterns among the concepts for the second theme support both the TAM and the FFM. This is not due to the association with most concepts from both conceptual models with the theme but rather with the patterns demonstrated among those concepts. Specifically, the personality types of agreeableness and extroversion coincided with perceptions of OPK usefulness. Moreover, neuroticism and conscientiousness did not. Because the agreeableness and extroversion personality types tend to see usefulness in a focal new technology (Ajibade, 2018;

Yu et al., 2005), the coincidence of these personality types with perceptions of OPK usefulness is supportive of both the TAM and the FFM.

In contrast, the patterns among concepts that constitute theme 3 are not extensively supportive of the TAM and the FFM. Specifically, the lack of a positive coincidence of the openness personality type and PU is counter to the results of prior studies of new technologies using both the TAM and the FFM (Ajibade, 2018; Yu et al., 2005). However, this finding may be a function of the type of new technology addressed in the current study, i.e., OPK products. As different samples and contexts may be used to develop further extant theory (Bamberger & Pratt, 2010), this discussion is reserved for Chapter 5.

Not all the themes were associated with both research questions. Specifically, themes 1 and 4 were associated with the first research question, and themes 2 and 3 were associated with the second research question. Table 5 presents the research questions vis-à-vis the themes. The decision rule for associating a theme with a research question was that the theme and research question shared one or more concepts from the theoretical framework. The decision rule supports the concept that a focal theme supports the TAM or the FFM. The association of concepts from the TAM or FFM does not lead to the conclusion of support for one or both components of the theoretical framework. Instead, the patterns among the TAM and the FFM concepts must be similar to what these conceptual models posit, and past research has supported the models. The conclusion is discussed in chapter 5.

Summary

In this chapter, the findings of the inductive thematic analysis procedures were reviewed, as guided by Braun and Clarke (2006). A total of 19 codes were developed, which resulted in eight categories. A total of four themes were identified in the inductive thematic analysis procedures, which included *personality factors via OPK characteristics, perceived ease of use (PEOU) via platform characteristics, perceived usefulness (PU) via the value of OPK,* and *use of OPK via challenges of OPK.* In this chapter, each of these themes was discussed in association with participant quotes. In the preceding chapter, Chapter 5, the implications of these findings with empirical research and theoretical knowledge are discussed. In Chapter 5, the researcher reviews recommendations for research and practice based on the findings presented in this chapter.

Chapter 5: Implications, Recommendations, and Conclusions

The problem in this study addressed the question of how personality traits of consumers

perceive value of OPK products using perceived usefulness (PU) and perceived ease of use

(PEOU) as constructs among consumers in the United States (Bahl et al., 2019; Fu et al., 2020;

Jin et al., 2020; Jing et al., 2020; Seibert et al., 2021; Su et al., 2019). Su et al. (2019) cited the

need for further inquiry to understand how perceived value in the OPK market is affected by

personality traits. Similarly, Bahl et al. (2019) and Seibert et al. (2021) expressed a need for

further research on more specific technologies related to personality traits rather than technology

in general. Several studies have called for further research on the TAM model, including

investigating user perspectives in e-learning (Mohammadi, 2015) and further exploration of

product characteristics: service quality, information quality, and system quality (Jin, 2020). In a

study on knowledge products in China, Fu et al. (2020) suggested future research on knowledge

products and consumer satisfaction from other countries. Failure to understand personality traits

within the constructs of OPK characteristics as well as their perception of value could result in

failed marketing strategies among digital entrepreneurs as competition in the OPK market

continues to grow (Beig et al., 2019; Fu et al., 2020; Kraus, 2018; Marbach et al., 2016;

Matarazzo, 2021; Su et al., 2019).

The purpose of this qualitative case study was to examine how different personality traits

describe value within the constructs of PU and PEOU of online courses in the OPK market using

the contextual antecedents of OPK characteristics of consumers in the United States from 2018–

2021. Usakli (2019) called for further research on personality traits in online shopping using a

qualitative method. They further suggested that studies should be expanded beyond higher

education and use students predominantly in research. Zhou et al. (2022) suggested that future studies focus on consumer characteristics in electronic commerce. Understanding consumer's personality traits within the OPK market constructs of OPK product characteristics helps identify consumer preferences and their PU and PEOU (Barnett, 2015).

The inductive thematic analysis of the textual data, following the recommendations and research methods of Braun and Clarke (2006), resulted in four total themes: *personality factors vis-a-vis OPK characteristics, perceived ease of use (PEOU) vis-a-vis platform characteristics, perceived usefulness (PU) vis-a-vis the value of OPK,* and *use of OPK vis-a-vis challenges of* OPK. Chapter 5 illustrates the implication of the results discussed in Chapter 4.

This discussion addresses the implications of how the themes address the research questions for the extant research, theory, the problem that motivated the study, and the potential significance of the results. Recommendations for future research and practice are reserved for this chapter's following two sections. The chapter concludes with a summary of the study, the importance of the study in relation to the theoretical framework, and the problem addressed. The concluding summary includes a conclusive "take home" message regarding the results as they pertain to fellow academics, practitioners, OPK businesses, and OPK consumers.

Implications of Themes by Research Questions

In this chapter, the researcher presents the implications of the findings presented in Chapter 4. Each of the themes is reviewed in relationship to empirical research. Additionally, the finding's relationship with the guiding theoretical framework is also discussed. The following sections are divided by each theme. The following sections discuss each of the associated research questions in terms of resultant textual data. Figure 9 also summarizes the relationship between research questions and the resultant themes derived from textual data.

Figure 9

Research Questions and Associated Themes

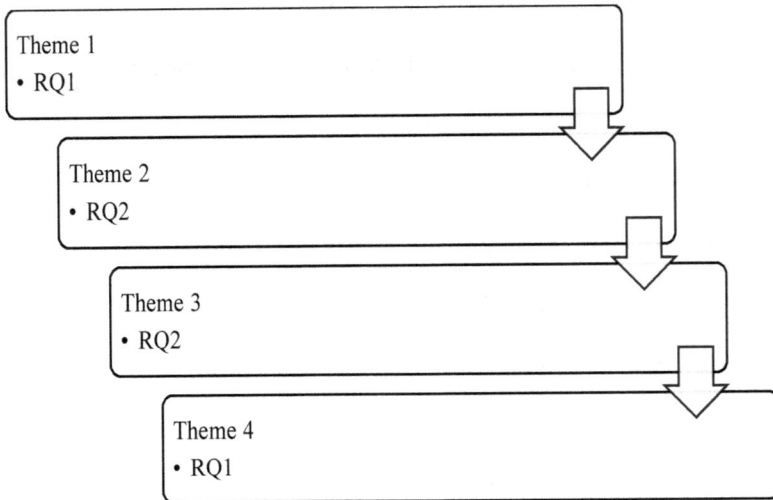

Theme 1
• RQ1

Theme 2
• RQ2

Theme 3
• RQ2

Theme 4
• RQ1

Research Question 1

RQ1 asked: How do the five personality trait factors (agreeableness, openness, neuroticism, conscientiousness and extroversion) impact consumer perception of online course characteristics (system quality, information quality and service quality)?

The responses from the participants formed two themes that established answers to research question 1. Themes 1 and 4 explained how the five personality trait factors impacted consumer perception of online course characteristics. Data from theme 1 also addressed research question one regarding how personality trait factors impact consumer perception of online course characteristics, which included information quality, service quality, and system quality. The findings of theme 1 expand upon previous understandings of OPK products in terms of applicability to individuals based on preference, learning needs, and the characteristics of the platforms. The findings from this theme offer the opportunity for researchers and practitioners to expand upon an understanding of ease of use and usefulness to the framework of individual personality and needs.

Information in theme 4 was used to address research question one regarding how personality may play a key role in the choice, ease, and use of OPK products. Data from theme 4 also addressed research question one regarding how individual preferences may impact consumer perception of online course characteristics, such as information quality, service quality, and system quality. The findings of the theme were critical in demonstrating the potential challenges and factors that influence OPK product use. Factors such as accountability and credibility were considered as added information that contributes to literature on the topic of OPK products. Additionally, these factors add to the TAM framework by demonstrating how such factors may ultimately influence individual consumers' perception of the use of OPK products.

Theme 1 (RQ1): Personality Factors via OPK Characteristics.

Data from theme 1 illustrated the importance of personality factors in terms of how participants perceived OPK characteristics. Participants reflected on their experiences with platforms, instructors, and personal preferences in OPK knowledge delivery. The findings of theme 1 were integral to understanding how personality may play a key role in the choice, ease, and usefulness of OPK products. Information from this theme expanded upon previous research findings regarding OPK product characteristics, platform, and individual factors as reported by participants. An individual's personality, preferences, and learning needs serve a key role in how participants reflect upon the characteristics of OPK platforms and the knowledge gained.

Participants in theme 1 emphasized that OPK usage varied based on their learning preferences. How participants delivered and received information was also critical in identifying if an OPK product was helpful for their personal needs. Previous researchers corroborated the importance of participants' PU and PEOU in considering the value and service of OPK products (Bahl et al., 2019; Fu et al., 2020; Jin & Xu, 2020; Jing et al., 2020; Su et al., 2019; Usakli, 2019). The current study expanded upon previous research by demonstrating that personality may be a crucial factor in how OPK product characteristics are perceived by individuals using such platforms. Data from this study also provided further information that illustrated the importance of individual characteristics of a learning platform in terms of how participants perceive these characteristics.

Participants discussed relevant factors such as material organization, preference toward an instructor or platform, and previous experience with online learning. Participants also discussed various characteristics of OPK products. Data from Holbrook (2006) and Hsiao (2021) supported these findings and demonstrated the importance of consumers' knowledge of the platform, material organization, as well as the aesthetic value of platforms in terms of the use of an OPK products. The current study confirmed previous research by demonstrating that participants hold varying perceptions of platform organization of knowledge, which can potentially influence how they perceive a platform's applicability and value.

Quality and service were two central characteristics of OPK products that participants discussed in this study. Participants reviewed platform quality's influence on using a product more frequently. Additionally, service was critical in terms of gaining a sufficient understanding of the material organization, the ability to delineate the goals of the platform service, and how information was delivered via prerecorded lectures or even live chats with educators. Similar to all products offered in an economic space (Khan, 2020; Taufique & Vaithiananthan, 2018), the service of OPK products defines how individuals perceive the ability to use a platform effectively. In this theme, participants reflected on differing perceptions of how OPK product's service influenced their use of the platform. Differing perceptions and learning preferences were key in how products were perceived as ideal for information gain.

Theme 4 (RQ1): Use of OPK vis-a-vis Challenges of OPK.

Data from theme 4 illustrated the mediating effects of OPK products use when considering the challenges of the platforms and learning methods used by differing suppliers. In addition, data derived from theme 4 was useful in supplying new information to address a gap in previous literature regarding the potential mediating effects of OPK products, such as challenges surrounding instructors, engagement, accountability, and credibility. Findings from this theme also illustrated the particular importance of personalities and preferences of participants. Different perceptions of the platform, internal evaluations of how OPK products may be applied, and usability appear to be highly individualistic, which may influence how OPK products are used and perceived by consumer bases.

Participants felt that using OPK products were based on factors such as weighing the benefits, accountability, and credibility of the instructor. In addition, researchers have discussed the importance of creating a well-developed online learning space to ensure individuals gain desired outcomes based on goals (Agarwal, 2015; Berger et al., 2015; Huang, 2016; Li et al., 2017; Punj, 2015). However, research regarding accountability within OPK products and resultant use is less prominent in the reviewed literature available. The data from theme 3 provides information to expand research and practice in exploring the role of accountability from a quantitative and qualitative perspective in terms of the use of OPK products.

Credibility is also a factor that researchers such as Hinnawi and Mohammad (2018) and Lambrecht et al. (2017) noted that might potentially influence perceptions of use amongst consumers. Participants in this study corroborated these findings by emphasizing that the credibility of the educator and the platform played a role in how they perceived the usability and information gain of the platforms. The findings of this study also extended previous literature by illustrating that the knowledge of an educator before using an OPK product influences their perception of usability. Exploring credibility in future examinations may supply influential data to support online learners and OPK platforms.

Other participants felt that lower-priced products were potentially as useful as higher-priced products when considering how knowledge was applied. Research from Gallaugher et al. (2001) and Ahmed (2020) demonstrated that free samples of paid content could lead individuals to consume other OPK products. While previous research demonstrated that lower-cost products could be perceived differentially by various consumer bases, the findings of this study demonstrated that participants felt that the value and use of products were based more closely upon their goal, motivation, and factors such as accountability and feedback supplied through OPK platforms (Koch & Benlian, 2017; Zhang et al., 2019). However, the challenges of platforms, which were often higher in lower-cost products, did influence their perceptions of use.

Research Question 2

RQ2 asked: How do the five personality trait factors (agreeableness, openness, neuroticism, conscientiousness, extroversion) and the online course characteristics (system quality, information quality, service quality) affect consumer perceived value using the constructs of perceived usefulness (PU) and perceived ease of use (PEOU)?

Research question 2 was answered based on themes 2 and 3, which illustrated the importance of product characteristics in terms of perceived ease of use (theme 2) while illustrating that the PU of OPK product characteristics was influenced by their perceived value of the OPK product (theme 3). The findings of the second theme demonstrated that the usefulness of products was based upon individuals' understanding and ability to gain knowledge from platforms. Participants emphasized that the platform characteristics of OPK were central in assessing if a platform had a high or low perceived ease of use. The information gained was a crucial factor in how participants reported their final experience with perceived ease of use among OPK product characteristics.

Theme 2 (RQ 2): Perceived Ease of Use (PEOU) via Platform Characteristics.

Participants who appreciated the system characteristics and quality were more likely to respond positively regarding ease of use in OPK products. Platform characteristics were also identified by previous researchers in terms of how a specific tool, application, or online learning space could lead toward the perception of ease of use (Cai et al., 2020; Fang et al., 2021; Meng et al., 2021; Su et al., 2019). The TAM framework has also been used to assess OPK market characteristics and their influence on individuals' perceived ease of use (Xu et al., 2021; Zhang et al., 2020). The findings of this study expanded upon previous research by illustrating that system characteristics, such as quality, information gain, instructor, and platforms, were critical to individuals who reported perceived ease of use. These findings demonstrate that individual factors of the platform may influence how an OPK product is perceived as easy to use in online learning spaces.

Participants also emphasized that in some cases, dependent on the cost of the product, the ease of use did not fully dictate the product's value. Research from Gao (2021) and Hyatt et al. (2019) supported this finding by demonstrating that the cost of a product is mediated by consumers' perception of value and use. The current study demonstrated that ease of use might also be a mediating factor for the individual perception of an OPK product. Future researchers may expand upon this finding by assessing the interaction, or relationship, between ease of use and product cost and information gained as reported by consumers.

The characteristics of the platform, such as the instructor, were central in terms of assessing the usability of OPK and the ability to gain information that would later lead to their report of perceived ease of use (Ashraf et al., 2014; Bleier et al., 2019; Marbach et al., 2016; Marbach et al., 2019; RuBell et al., 2020). Product characteristics were also described by Mohamad et al. (2021) as a principal factor in terms of intent to use or purchase a product. Various factors, such as aesthetics, participant attitude, and information presentation, are critical to consumers' use of OPK products (Biucky & Harandi, 2017; Zhou et al., 2019). Information from this theme illustrated that participants have similar concerns over OPK product characteristics, but the ease of use may mediate challenges or dislikes experienced within the platform. Additionally, participants reported that their attempt to gain knowledge, end goal motivation, and passion for pursuing knowledge was central in overcoming perceptions of platform ease and resulting in the reported usability of the OPK product.

The second theme aided in addressing research question two regarding how personality trait factors are important when considering the online course characteristics (system quality, information quality, service quality) that affect consumer perceived value using the constructs of PU and PEOU. The information gained from this theme demonstrated the importance of exploring information gain, usefulness, and platform characteristics, such as instructors and platforms themselves, in terms of future research and practice. Data from this theme corroborated previous research regarding the importance of OPK characteristics while providing added information regarding how participants reported their perception of OPK characteristics in terms of their perceived ease of use.

Theme 3 (RQ 2): Perceived Usefulness (PU) via Value of OPK.

Each participant viewed platform value uniquely based on their experiences and goals. Platforms that provided ample learning opportunities, attentiveness to detail, and resources for learning were crucial to participant perceptions of usefulness. Participants' reflections in theme 3 demonstrated PU within a new understanding of how individuals uniquely perceived value based upon previous experiences, goals, and the information supplied, either tangible or intangible, through OPK platforms and products.

Participants also reflected that the value of OPK was not in the product cost or online platform alone. Many participants felt that OPK value was inherent to how the individual used, gained, or applied knowledge. Researchers demonstrated that the cost of a product might influence user perception of the value of the product (Mendoza et al., 2017; Yu et al., 2021). The same findings were reflected in this study, in which some participants felt that a lower-priced product would have a lower value. However, other participants emphasized that the user's intent in gaining information and completing a course was more important than price when assessing value. These findings demonstrate that individual personality and preferences may play a critical role in the PU and reported value of OPK products. Additionally, the finding corroborates previous researchers' emphasis that cost and personalities are critical antecedents to perceptions of usefulness and value (Mendoza et al., 2017; Yu et al., 2021). These results may expand upon the TAM framework by supplying information supporting the intersection between the perception of cost, user personality, and reported final value.

The third theme supplied data that addressed research question two regarding how personality trait actors are important when considering the online course characteristics (system quality, information quality, service quality) that affect consumer perceived value using the constructs of PU and PEOU. The data from this study corroborated findings regarding the importance of service quality through an expanded qualitative approach, which was absent and previous literature (Cai et al., 2020; Chen et al., 2021; Zhang & Wu, 2019). Research within this theme expanded upon the gap in the literature by demonstrating that consumer-based behaviors and personalities, based on individual preferences and goals, may play a role in the PU and reported value of OPK products.

Recommendations for Future Research and Practice

In this section, the recommendation for practice and research are presented. The presented recommendations, spanning accountability, the role of credibility, and employment of quantitative explorations, are potentially crucial to the improved understanding of perceived ease of use and usefulness when examining personality traits and consumption of OPK products. Figure 10 demonstrates an overview of the supplied recommendations for research and practice.

Figure 10

Recommendations for Research and Practice

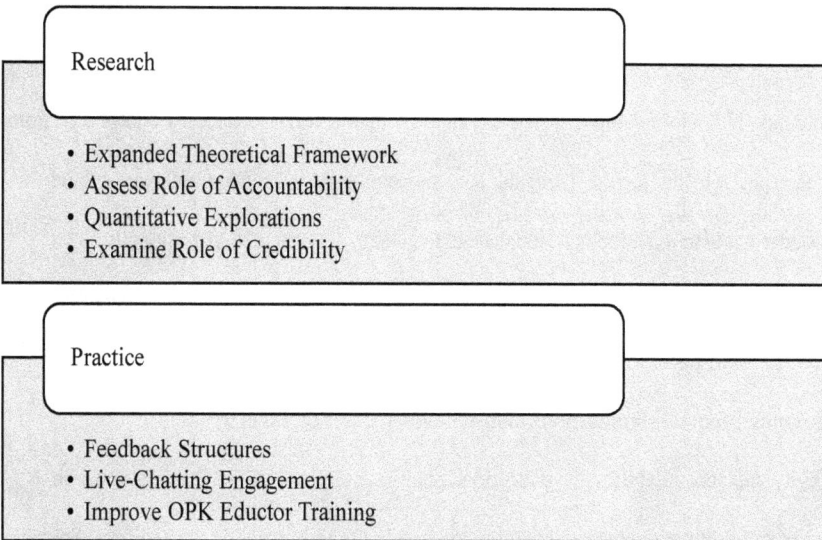

Research

- Expanded Theoretical Framework
- Assess Role of Accountability
- Quantitative Explorations
- Examine Role of Credibility

Practice

- Feedback Structures
- Live-Chatting Engagement
- Improve OPK Eductor Training

Recommendations for Future Research

The following recommendations for research are presented based on the information gained from the current dissertation and supported by the existing literature reviewed in Chapter 2. These recommendations were noted based on the findings of this research study, examination of the framework's application to this research, addressing a necessary need that this research did not note, observing different facets of usability and ease of use, and using a different method and research design. These recommendations are shared as they can further expand the research findings presented here. While the purpose of this study was to examine how different personality traits describe value within the constructs of PU and PEOU of online courses in the OPK market, future research would benefit the impact of use when observed using a framework(s) other than TAM or FFM. As TAM demonstrates how users come to adopt and use technology, guiding researchers in understanding that users, when presented with recent technology, are most likely to face a variety of factors that influence their ultimate decision to use the system, another framework could offer different perceptions from users (Chao, 2019; Davis, 1989; Straub, 2009). The use of such frameworks as Technological-Personal-Environmental (TPE), for example, delineates an individual level of technology acceptance from three noted aspects: technological, personal, and environmental. The TPE framework would offer a broader angle to examine individual-level technology acceptance. Additionally, comparing different platforms supplying OPK products could show such products' benefits, risks, and negative aspects.

Secondly, another significant recommendation focuses on examining the level of responsibility and accountability in a platform's usability, ease, and value. Existing research found that usability function and social ability are within the five stages of the decision-making process (Huang et al., 2017; Otero-Lopez et al., 2021). To further determine the aspect of accountability in OPK product's usability based on personality traits, it is recommended that further research focus on examining platforms supplying OPK products and may find improved accountability measures to increase the platform's usefulness and value as perceived by current and potential clients. Recommendations for research are to assess accountability regarding the role of perceived value and usefulness of OPK products. The findings of this study emphasize the importance of accountability in perceiving whether a product is valuable, useful, or easy to use. However, despite participants' reflections, it was unclear how strongly this may influence perceived ease of use and usefulness.

Future research on accountability may be an element that may aid in the development of consumer attraction for the platform supplying OPK products. Additionally, data from this methodology of using platforms can supply further opportunities for understanding the interaction between varying factors, such as personality and perceived ease of use and usefulness, when considering personality factors. Therefore, the researcher recommends, either through quantitative or qualitative research, further examination of the role of accountability in terms of the perceived value and usefulness of OPK products.

Thirdly, recommendations for future research suggested that researchers employ quantitative explorations, expanding upon the knowledge of OPK products in terms of perceived ease of use, usefulness, and personality traits. Exploring the quantitative relationship, if any, between certain personality traits and antecedents of online OPK product usage may foster the growth of platforms and consumer bases (Bagby & Widiger, 2018; Smith et al., 2019). In addition, further research using a quantitative methodology may supply information that offers extended generalizability and further expand upon the strength of different personality types in using OPK products.

Lastly, a recommendation for future research is to examine the instructor's or course's credibility in terms of the moderating factor of consumer perceived value and usefulness in OPK products. Participants in the study discussed the importance of credibility, of the platform, or the instructor, in terms of their perceived value and usefulness of the platform or product. Understanding the role of credibility may supply data that will support information for researchers and support the TAM model further. Lane (1993) argued that customer-based brand equity is most important for considering how individuals are loyal to a brand and are likely to purchase and stay within the company. Keller and Lehmann (2006) also recommended similar recommendations to Lane (1993). They argued that brands and branding processes must prioritize brand equity to understand the consumer base and mindset.

Recommendations for Practice

Recommendation for practice is shared based on the reviewed findings in Chapters 4 and 5 and supported with existing literature. The recommendations for practice are guided toward improving feedback, encouraging interactions with users, and supplying OPK instruction for educators. These recommendations for practice may be implemented to further improve consumer base usage, perception of ease of use, and usefulness amongst OPK users and businesses.

The first recommendation for practice is to implement improved feedback structures within OPK platforms. Participants in the study emphasized difficulty with gaining feedback or a lack of one-on-one mentoring with some specific instructional platforms. In addition, participants emphasized that their perceived ease of use and usefulness were influenced by feedback, lack of structures, and OPK platforms. Similarly, Van Popta et al. (2017) and Kalman (2014) found that with MOOC applications, the students were more likely to succeed if the instruction offered availability and support for user needs. Resultantly, the researcher encourages current or future OPK developers to assess how feedback may improve consumer perception and use of such products.

The second recommendation for practice is to assess how participants can interact with other peers or teachers of OPK products. Participants discussed the importance of live chatting, discussion, and feedback from other colleagues on the same platforms. For some participants, the ability to live chat was critical in terms of how they perceived the used or value of the product. Perceived value involves interaction between the consumer and the subject or product (Holbrook, 2006; Hsiao, 2021). A consumer's intention to purchase knowledge products relies on knowledge received, as well as organization, selection, interpretation of knowledge, and the value they expect to receive (Hosta & Zabkar, 2021; Su et al., 2017; Su et al., 2019; Seibert et al., 2021). Online consumer engagement and aesthetic value are related to an easy-to-use layout and are directly related to perceived value (Ashraf et al., 2014; Bleier et al., 2019; Marbach et al., 2016; Marbach et al., 2019; RuBell et al., 2020). As a result, practitioners should consider how participants engage with OPK products. Platform developers may find that added feedback and communication can foster further use of online learning products.

The third recommendation for practice is to assess and improve instruction training for OPK educators. As the OPK market grows substantially, a new influx of educators is seeking the best means of teaching their specific advice or knowledge to potential consumers. Practitioners may consider how to best implement instruction that engages participants. Korepin et al. (2020) supported this by noting a need to transform e-learning further to meet the new market requirements for training specializations in digital logistics. As such, this learning and training capability needs to be examined to determine what level of training impacts instructor success. Participants in the study reflected on the importance of engaging and non-judgmental individuals that teach information on OPK platforms. Failure to ensure appropriate educator means of instructing students may result in declining growth or usage of an OPK product.

Recommendation Summary

The recommendations for future research and practice implied in this study contend that expanding the literary knowledge-base and increasing informational and more vital practices with OPK product use have far-reaching ability to improve this field of study and discipline. Therefore, the next logical step should include pursuing and explaining these recommendations for future research and practices with academics, practitioners, and experts in these technological fields.

Limitations and Recommendations for Research and Practice

As with any research, particularly qualitative research, the number of participants is limited due to the scope of the project. Further research could include expanding the number of participants and studying participants and their personality traits within the TAM framework over a more extended period.

Conclusions

In this chapter, the researcher discussed the findings of the study. A total of four themes were identified with this dissertation, including *personality factors vis-a-vis OPK characteristics, perceived ease-of-use (PEOU) vis-a-vis platform characteristics, perceived usefulness (PU) vis-a-vis the value of OPK, and use of OPK vis-a-vis challenges of OPK*. The four themes were used to elucidate information that corroborated and expanded previous literature within the study's theoretical framework. Data obtained from the textual information supplied by participants prove helpful in understanding how to expand upon research regarding OPK platform usage through understanding the role of PU, PEOU, and the personality factors of OPK consumer bases.

The problem in this study addressed the question of how personality traits of consumers perceive value of OPK products using perceived usefulness (PU) and perceived ease of use (PEOU) as constructs among consumers in the United States (Bahl et al., 2019; Fu et al., 2020; Jin et al., 2020; Jing et al., 2020; Seibert et al., 2021; Su et al., 2019). While a plethora of research from Bahl et al. (2019), Fu et al. (2020), Jin et al. (2020), Jing et al. (2020), Seibert et al. (2021), and Su et al. (2019) focused on similar research, many of these experts claimed a need for further inquiry to understanding how perceived value in the OPK market is affected by personality traits.

Such existing literature examined the behavior patterns of online shoppers that included a willingness to purchase and purchase intention factors, such as perceived risk, perceived value, and perceived use (Berger et al., 2015; Biucky et al., 2017; Bucko et al., 2018; Gvili et al., 2020; Ha et al., 2019; Li et al., 2017; Rajani, 2019). The problem was limited literature research examining personality traits and technology interaction with digital learning products sold by for-profit businesses (Bento et al., 2019; Bruso et al., 2020; Regele, 2020; Zhou, 2022). The problem was addressed based on the results of this study, which were conveyed in four major themes: the personality factors via OPK characteristics, perceived ease of use via platform characteristics, perceived usefulness via the value of OPK, and use of OPK via challenges of OPK.

The study's findings uniquely added to the literature by providing a better understanding of how personality influences the usage of OPK products in terms of value, ease, and usefulness. Additionally, the responses and participant perceptions provided an understanding of how personality traits of consumer's perceived value of OPK products impacted the use of PU and PEOU among consumers in the United States. Exploring how personality factors (agreeableness, openness, conscientiousness, neuroticism and extroversion) impacted consumer's perceived value, PU, and PEOU within the contextual antecedents of OPK characteristics provided further understanding and knowledge that value, usefulness, and ease of use are vital in the success of a product. Consumer personality traits are impactful in value, usefulness, and perceived ease of use when considering OPK products and should be considered for future practice with OPK sales and implementation.

The results of this study presented an understanding of practice by addressing how different personality traits describe value within the constructs of PU and PEOU of online courses in the OPK market using the contextual antecedents of OPK characteristics of consumers in the United States from 2018–2021. In addition, the explanation provided further understanding of how consumers' personality traits in the OPK market within the constructs of OPK product characteristics may help identify consumer preferences and their PU and PEOU. Recognizing how value is a significant motivator for consumer purchasing and examining how personality traits impact this value, organizational leaders may understand perceptions regarding the value of PU and PEOU of online courses.

www.ingramcontent.com/pod-product-compliance
Lightning Source LLC
Chambersburg PA
CBHW071644210326
41597CB00017B/2104